WRITING
A
RESEARCH
PAPER

FOURTH EDITION

JONATHA CEELY
HELEN W. DUNN
MARY TYLER KNOWLES
JUDITH ROBBINS

Longman
New York & London

W9-CYG-668

To Arlene Rubin, an unfailing resource

Writing a Research Paper, Fourth Edition

Copyright © 1992, 1983, 1978
by Jonatha Ceely, Helen W. Dunn, Mary Tyler Knowles, Judith Robbins.

Longman, 10 Bank Street, White Plains, N.Y. 10606

Associated companies:
Longman Group Ltd., London
Longman Cheshire Pty., Melbourne
Longman Paul Pty., Auckland
Copp Clark Longman Ltd., Toronto

Senior editor: Lyn McLean
Production editor: Marcy Gray
Text design: Kevin Kall
Cover design: Susan J. Moore
Production supervisor: Anne Armeny

ISBN: 0-8013-0698-1

3 4 5 6 7 8 9 10-CRS-98 97 96 95 94

Contents

Preface

Writing a research paper is not a single action but a series of interlocked steps, a process. Throughout this brief manual it has been our aim to define this process and to give reasons for including each step. The students who use this manual thoughtfully, understanding and mastering each stage of the paper-writing process, should acquire a tool they can employ in any discipline that requires written work. It is our hope that students will discover that a system, a structure, can liberate rather than restrict, for we believe that mastering the means of communication is but a step toward a more important goal—the free exchange of ideas.

The idea for this manual has been developed over several years. We are grateful to the Language Arts Summer Workshop, Lexington Public Schools, Lexington, Massachusetts, whose work helped us as we began to teach our own Expository Writing course. As we prepared the material for this manual, we became increasingly aware of the debt of gratitude we owe for the goodwill and support we have received from many people. We particularly thank Arlene Rubin, who indefatigably provided material on the use of the library, the Winsor School for providing the setting in which we could develop and test our material, and, finally, all of our students for their thoughtful and courteous responses to both the strengths and weaknesses in this material as it developed over the past twelve years.

THE
RESEARCH
PROCESS

I
Selecting a Worthwhile Subject

A. THE CHOICE OF TOPIC

It is not necessary to choose for your research paper a topic on which you are already well informed; rather, choose an area about which you are curious and wish to know more. When a possible subject occurs to you, investigate the resources of the libraries that are available to you and begin a tentative bibliography. (See IIIA) This activity serves three purposes. First, it reveals whether experts have already treated your topic so thoroughly that you would be merely repeating their research. Second, it reveals whether the topic is so limited or so esoteric that there is insufficient material on it. Third, it reveals whether the material is merely popular and superficial.

B. THE FACTUAL RESEARCH PAPER

The topic chosen and the kind of material available on it will tend to determine whether the final paper is a factual or problem-centered paper. If, for example, you wish to write about American Indian craft techniques or the life cycle of a turtle, you will probably find that your final paper is essentially descriptive in its presentation of material. Of course, you will need to develop a clear thesis that limits and focuses your research, but you will rely on the assertions of experts rather than on your own analysis of primary sources as you support that thesis. Thus, the factual paper brings together reliable information and the ideas of recognized experts in order to define and describe an area of knowledge. (See Appendixes A and B for examples of factual research papers.)

C. THE PROBLEM-CENTERED RESEARCH PAPER

A problem-centered paper seeks a solution to a problem. The problem-centered paper has these characteristics: recognizing a problem, stating an hypothesis, analyzing it, presenting data from a variety of sources, and coming to a conclusion inferred from the data presented. Based on investigation and the weighing of valid research materials, this conclusion should be the major emphasis of the paper and should be the writer's own. Thus, the problem-centered paper differs from the factual paper even though both require substantial research, and both may seek answers to a question. The problem-centered paper has a conclusion which may involve any of the following: assessment, analysis, evaluation, or interpretation. Whereas the factual paper is largely an exercise in compiling and reporting facts, the problem-centered paper goes one step further by making valid inferences or presenting conclusions clearly drawn from the data presented. See Appendix C for an example of a problem-centered paper written by a student who uses particularly sophisticated vocabulary and syntax to express her ideas.

D. NEED FOR AN EARLY AND CLEAR STATEMENT OF TOPIC

Because you will not be able to handle the research process efficiently if your topic is too broad, limit and clearly state the topic as a phrase or sentence as soon as possible. The narrowing process might proceed in this way:

> General area of interest: Significant 20th Century American Women
> General topic: Eleanor Roosevelt
> Limited topic: How Eleanor Roosevelt changed from a dependent to an independent woman

In exploring your general area of interest you might read widely in several anthologies, but your research for this paper will begin with a biography of Eleanor Roosevelt and then be further limited to particular periods or incidents in her life.

The process of narrowing the topic of a factual paper is similar:

> General area of interest: Ecology
> General topic: The Salt Marsh
> Limited topic: How the balanced ecosystem of the salt marsh is vulnerable to pollution

If the limited topic is developed primarily by the use of description, it will be a factual paper. Notice, however, that the line between the factual and the problem-centered paper can be a very fine one. The treatment you choose for your topic will depend on the kind of material your research reveals and the approach to it that you prefer. What remains essential is that the broad, fuzzy general topic be narrowed to a clearly defined, concisely stated limited topic. Do not hesitate as your research progresses to shift the emphasis or refine the wording of your limited topic; do be sure that at all times the scope of your research and the statement of limited topic are precisely and logically linked.

II

Using the Library: Sources for Assembling a Bibliography

Begin your research by looking up your general topic in library catalogs, periodical and newspaper indexes, and the major encyclopedias. Try to find as many and as varied sources as possible, always realizing that magazines, newspapers, pictures, movies, television programs, and telephone and face-to-face interviews are often sources quite as valuable as bound books. If catalogs and indexes do not show books or articles on your topic, go back to your general area of interest. For example, if you find nothing under the heading "Salt Marsh," go back to the general heading of "Ecology." Be flexible and imaginative in thinking of catalog headings under which material of interest to you might be filed.

A. LIBRARY CATALOGS

Although it may be in one of several forms (cards, books, microfilm, electronic), the main function of the library catalog is to indicate which specific books the library has on your topic.

1. Card Catalogs—A card catalog lists every book in the library by author, title, and general subject on individual file cards. In addition, on the left-hand side of each file card is a number showing the location of the book in the library. Jot down the call numbers of promising books and browse in the section(s) of the library where the books are shelved. Much valuable information can be located in this way.
2. Book Catalogs—A book catalog gives the same information as a card catalog but in book form.
3. Microfilm Catalogs—A microfilm catalog uses film to list every book in a library by author, title, and general subject; each film entry is read by looking at the screen of a film reader. The call number will be at the bottom of each film entry.
4. Electronic Catalogs—Computer catalogs (sometimes called on-line or public-access catalogs) are often found in public and college libraries. These computer catalogs provide information by asking the researcher

either to choose topics from a menu format or to type in the name of an author, a book title, or a general subject heading. The citations for relevant books or articles will then appear on the computer screen. There is no single format for such catalogs; however, they tend to be easy to use because they present the researcher with instructions to follow.

B. ENCYCLOPEDIAS

You may wish to begin your research by consulting an encyclopedia, for a well-edited encyclopedia is an excellent tool for research. First, it will let you know whether your general topic is an appropriate heading under which to find information. Second, it will give you an overview of your subject and indicate whether it is one that is worth further exploration. *Use only one encyclopedia as a source.* The synopsis of a subject provided by most encyclopedias is useful, but the body of your research must go beyond such a general approach.

1. *Encyclopedia Americana*—Excellent for all North American topics as well as for scientific and technical topics. Includes biographies of living people and essays on individual works of art, music, and literature. Frequently updated.
2. *The New Encyclopedia Britannica*—More scholarly, but more difficult to use because it has two separate parts, the Micropedia (brief coverage of selected topics) and the Macropedia (coverage of topics in depth). You *must* use the index to find all the information on your topic as well as where in The Encyclopedia this information is located. Truly international in scope and contains more biographies than any other encyclopedia.
3. *Collier's Encyclopedia*—Easiest to understand of these three encyclopedias and the most heavily indexed. Particularly good for current economic conditions and problems; includes analysis as well as facts. Comprehensive 12,000-item bibliography in the last volume in addition to shorter bibliographies at the end of many of the articles.
4. Specialized Encyclopedias—*Encyclopedia of Bioethics, McGraw-Hill Encyclopedia of World Biography, International Encyclopedia of the Social Sciences, McGraw-Hill Encyclopedia of Science and Technology, Notable American Women,* etc.

Be sure to consult the index volume when using any multi-volume set of encyclopedias in order to find all possible references to your topic and to related topics. Also be aware of the helpful bibliographies which usually appear at the end of longer articles.

C. PERIODICAL INDEXES

For most current topics, articles in periodicals will be useful. To find such articles, consult general and specialized book indexes, film indexes, electronic indexes and, for the most recent information, on-line databases.

1. *Reader's Guide to Periodical Literature*—Indexes the majority of popular magazines and is the best known and most generally available. It is, however, not the best source to consult for a specialized topic.
2. *Access: The Supplementary Index to Periodicals*—Designed to complement *Reader's Guide. Access* includes only those magazines not included in the *Reader's Guide* list. It also indexes regional and city magazines.
3. *Magazine Index*—A film and electronic index to general magazines that combines the most popular titles from *Reader's Guide* and *Access;* useful for book, theater, art reviews, and current information. Updated monthly.
4. *Art Index*—Indexes art publications of all types including yearbooks and museum bulletins; also includes entries for reproductions of works of art and book reviews. (For the teaching of art, also consult *Education Index.*)
5. *Biography Index*—Indexes biographical information in books, periodicals, pamphlets, prefaces, and the *New York Times* obituaries. Includes an index to occupations and professions.
6. *Education Index*—Indexes magazines, yearbooks, and monographs. Subjects include education, learning psychology, and physical education.
7. *General Science Index*—Begun in 1978, this index provides a guide to scientific, medical, and technical periodicals and journals at a more accessible level than *Applied science and Technology Index.*
8. *Humanities Index* (formerly *Social Sciences and Humanities Index*) —Indexes area studies, folklore, history, language and literature, performing arts, philosophy, religion and theology, journalism, motion picture reviews, and book reviews.
9. *P.A.I.S. (Public Affairs Information Service)*—Indexes publications on all subjects having to do with contemporary public issues and public policy. Included are economics, history, political science, and sociology. Publications indexed include magazines, books, government documents, and reports on public and private organizations. Also available on-line.
10. *Social Sciences Index* (formerly *Social Sciences and Humanities Index.*)—Includes anthropology, economics, geography, law and criminology, political science, psychology, social work and public welfare, sociology, and urban studies. Also includes book reviews pertaining to these subjects.

Many, if not all, of the above indexes are published both electronically and in hard copy. Libraries may subscribe to either form; check with the reference librarian.

D. NEWSPAPER INDEXES

For the most current approach to a topic, consult your daily newspaper or on-line news databases. Access to previously published articles may also be obtained from databases or newspaper indexes in book form.

1. *The New York Times Index*—Gives summaries of important news, editorials and features published in the *New York Times.*
2. *Wall Street Journal Index*—Indexes current business and economic information as it appears in the *Wall Street Journal.*
3. Local newspaper indexes. Most city newspapers maintain indexes but public access is very limited. Libraries frequently have indexes for the larger newspapers and may also subscribe to on-line data banks which include newspaper indexing. For example, the *Washington Post* and the *Los Angeles Times* are available on-line; *The Boston Globe Index* is available in book form.

Many libraries have open-stack systems, and thus you can browse in the areas appropriate to your topic. Use the catalog to find the call numbers for several books; then examine the shelves for further pertinent materials. Look not only at the title of a book in your subject area but also at its table of contents and index to determine whether there will be chapters relevant to your research.

When using any library, remember that the function of a librarian is to assist the public as well as to take care of the materials. ASK if you cannot find what you need.

III

Making a Bibliography

A working bibliography is a compilation of sources which you think will be useful in researching your subject; it consists of index cards on each of which you have recorded information about *one* likely source. This information will help you keep track of your sources during the research process and will be useful later in writing the final bibliography for the finished paper.

As you consult library catalogs and indexes for possible material, be sure that the sources you actually include in your working bibliography are both available and pertinent to your topic. Because information on scientific subjects is continually being updated and because methods of historical and biographical research change, your bibliography should consist primarily of sources published within the last twenty-five years (check publication date); however, you should not overlook earlier definitive works in your subject area, nor should you fail to include primary sources when appropriate.

Not only must your sources be timely, but also your authors must be competent in their respective fields. There are several ways of determining competence:

1. Check format of the book itself. Does it have footnotes, bibliography, and index?
2. See what information is given on the jacket, in the preface, or in the introduction about the author. What is the author's experience and expertise?
3. See whether the work occurs in the bibliographies of other books in the same field.

BE AWARE THAT THERE MAY BE A VARIETY OF POINTS OF VIEW ON YOUR TOPIC.

A. THE FORM FOR THE BIBLIOGRAPHY ENTRY

You must be consistent in the form you use to record bibliographical information. While there are various correct ways of writing bibliography entries, the Modern Language Association (MLA) recommendations which provide guidelines for this manual are widely accepted. The bibliography entry consists of the following parts:

1. Author (or editor).
2. Title (of book or article).
3. Publication facts:
   a. for books: city, publisher(s), date
   b. for encyclopedias: name, edition, and/or year
   c. for periodicals: title, volume or number for a scholarly journal, date, pages.

These divisions are separated by periods. The necessary information will be on the title page and on the back of the title page. If some information is not given, write n.d. (for *no data available*) in the appropriate place in the entry. *Be sure to record all data in correct bibliographic form.*

B. WRITING A BIBLIOGRAPHY CARD

Following the appropriate form in the examples below, make a bibliography card for every useful source; be sure to do each card completely, in ink. In a few cases, the examples and following directives call for more information than is required for a formal bibliography entry (e.g., volume and page of an encyclopedia article) because you may need to refer to this information again. The sample bibliography entries in Section III C provide models for the types of sources which you will encounter most frequently. If you need to record a source for which no model is provided, consult the current edition of the *MLA Handbook for Writers of Research Papers.*
   It is *absolutely essential* that you code each bibliography card at the upper right-hand corner. The code for each source consists of the first letter of the author's last name followed by the first letter of the first word of the title, excluding *a, an,* and *the.* You will use these code designations on your note cards to identify the sources which you have used in your research. Also, note in parentheses at the lower right corner the library from which you borrowed the book. Additionally, you may find it useful to write the library call number at the lower left.

General Model

```
                          Code
Author. Title.
Place: Publisher, date.

Library              (Library)
Call Number
```

For a Complete Book

```
                          CM
Cook, Fred J. Maverick: Fifty
Years of Investigative
Reporting. New York: G. P.
Putnam's Sons, 1984.

(070.9        (Wellesley Library)
Coo)
```

For an Item in a Collection

```
                          LW
Liska, George. "War and
Order." Globalism and Its
Critics. Ed. William Taubman.
Lexington, MA: D. C. Heath
and Co., 1973. 40–52.
(E840
.T38)                    (BPL)
```

For an Unsigned Magazine Article

```
                          PA
"Presidential Commission
Cites Improvements in
European Airport and Airway
Safety." Aviation Week 26 Feb.
1990: 31
                    (Newton Free
                       Library)
```

For a Signed Encyclopedia Entry

```
                          WW
Wright, Esmond. "Washington,
George." Collier's Encyclo-
pedia. Vol. 23. 1987 ed. 282–
289.

              (Winsor Library)
```

For a Signed Newspaper Item

```
                          BA
Buckley, Tom. "Anyone for
War?" Rev. of The Long Gray
Line by Rick Atkinson. The
New York Times Book Review
22 Oct. 1989: 18.
                       (NYPL)
```

C. BIBLIOGRAPHY SAMPLES

The following is a series of bibliography samples, not a formal bibliography. A formal bibliography is arranged in alphabetical order by author's last name.

1. Printed Works
  a. Single Works
  1) *Book by one author*
  Cook, Fred J. Maverick: Fifty Years of Investigative Reporting. New York: G. P. Putnam's Sons, 1984.
  2) *Another book by the same author*
  ———. The Ku Klux Klan: America's Recurring Nightmare. Englewood Cliffs, NJ: J. Messner, 1980.
  3) *Book by two authors*
  Manley, Sean, and Susan Belcher. O, Those Extraordinary Women! Philadelphia: Chilton Book Co., 1972.
  4) *Book by three or more authors*
  Masterton, William L., et al. Chemical Principles. Philadelphia: Saunders College Publishing, 1985.
  5) *Edited work of one author*
  Lawrence, D. H. Complete Poems. Eds. Vivian de Sola Pinto and F. Warren Roberts. New York: Viking Press, 1971.
  6) *Translation*
  Cortazar, Julio. Around the Day in Eighty Worlds. Trans. Thomas Christensen. San Francisco: North Point Press, 1986.
  7) *Corporate Author*
  American Medical Association. The American Medical Association's Handbook of First Aid and Emergency Care. New York: Random House, 1980.
  8) *Conference Proceedings*
  Proceedings of the 1985 State Fish and Wildlife Directors Conference. 4–6 June 1985. Washington, DC: U.S. Department of Commerce, National Marine Fisheries Service, 1986.
  9) *Occasional report*
  Mendelsohn, Everett. A Human Reconstruction of Science. A report prepared for a conference on women. Cambridge, MA: Radcliffe Institute, April 1972.
  b. Collections
  1) *Previously published work in a collection*
  Fox, Paula. "News from the World." Confrontation (Spring 1975): 78–81. Rpt. in Short Shorts: An Anthology of the Shortest Stories. Eds. Irving Howe and Ilana Wiener Howe. Boston: David R. Godine, 1982. 242–247.
  2) *Work in an edited collection*
  Liska, George. "War and Order." Globalism and Its Critics. Ed. William Taubman. Lexington, MA: D. C. Heath and Co., 1973. 40–52.
  3) *Edited collection from which two or more works have been cited*
  Williams, Robert H., ed. To Live and To Die: When, Why and How. New York: Springer-Verlag, 1973.

c. Encyclopedias

    1) *Signed article in an encyclopedia*

    Wright, Esmond. "Washington, George." Collier's Encyclopedia
        1987 ed.

    2) *Unsigned article in an encyclopedia*

    "Icarus." Encyclopedia Americana. 1989 ed.

d. Revisions and Republications

    1) *Reprint or facsimile of an earlier edition*

    Braddon, Mary Elizabeth. Lady Audley's Secret. 1887. New York:
        Dover, 1974.

    2) *Reprint with new foreword, afterword or introduction*

    Crane, Stephen. The Red Badge of Courage. 1895. Afterword by
        Clifton Fadiman.

    3) *Edition other than the first*

    Baum, Lawrence. The Supreme Court. 3rd ed. Washington, DC:
        Congressional Quarterly Press, 1989.

e. Magazines, Journals and Newspapers

    1) *Signed magazine article*

    Murphy, Cait. "Hong Kong: A Culture of Emigration." The Atlantic
        Apr. 1991: 20–26.

    2) *Unsigned magazine article*

    "Presidential Commission Cites Improvements in European Air-
        port and Airway Safety." Aviation Week 26 Feb. 1990: 31.

    3) *Journal article*

    Mendelson, Edward. "Word Processing: A Guide for the Perplexed."
        Yale Review 74 (1985): 615–640.

    4) *Unsigned newspaper article showing edition*

    "Alaska Oil by Land and Sea." New York Times 17 July 1977, nat'l
        ed.: A4.

f. Government Documents

    1) *Printed by Government Printing Office*

      a) *Report by a government department*

    United States. Bureau of Labor Statistics. A Brief History of the
        American Labor Movement. 1970 ed. Washington, DC: GPO,
        1970.

      b) *Report of hearings*

    United States. Congress. Senate. Committee on Government Oper-
        ations. Subcommittee on Intergovernmental Relations. Com-
        mittee on the Judiciary. Subcommittees on Separation of
        Powers and on Administrative Practice and Procedure. Hear-
        ings. 93rd Congress, 1st session. 12 vols. Washington, DC:
        GPO, 1946.

    2) *Printed by private publisher*

    United States. National Advisory Commission on Civil Disorders.
        Report of the National Advisory Commission on Civil Disor-
        ders. New York Times Edition. New York: E.P. Dutton, 1969.

g. Reviews
    1) *Book*
    Buckley, Tom. "Anyone for War?" Rev. of The Long Gray Line by
        Rick Atkinson. The New York Times Book Review 22 Oct.
        1989: 18.
    2) *Exhibition*
    Sherman, Mary. "Expressionist Barlach's Strong, Solitary Fig-
        ures." Rev. of Ernst Barlach. Pucker Safrai Gallery, Boston.
        Boston Globe 22 Feb. 1990: 76.
    3) *Performance*
    Kelly, Kevin. "An Open Letter to 'Love Letters.'" Rev. of Love Let-
        ters, by A. R. Gurney. Wilbur Theater, Boston. Boston Globe 22
        Feb. 1990: 73+.

h. Indirect Sources
If you cannot find the original source, but must use material quoted
or summarized within another book (the indirect source), your
bibliography card should give all information available about
the original source. It should also give full information about
the indirect source. All this material will be necessary for your
footnotes. The formal bibliography entry in your paper will
give only the information about the indirect source. For example, on one bibliography card record *both:*

> **a)** Broehl, Wayne G. The Molly Maguires. Cambridge,
> MA: Harvard University Press, 1964. [**Indirect Source**]
> **b)** Marvin Schegel, Ruler of the Reading: The Life of
> Franklin B. Gowan. Harrisburg: Archives Publishing
> Co. of Pennsylvania, 1947: 72, qtd. in Broehl 206. [**Di-
> rect Source**]

You will include only (a) in the bibliography of your paper but
will need both (a) and (b) for making footnotes. See sample
footnote[27] in Section VII: Preparing The Final Draft.

2. Other Media
a. Television or Radio Programs
    Private Lives, Public Trust. Writ. Stephen Schlow. Dir. Dimitri
        Miades. CBS. WHDH, Boston, 27 June 1990.
b. Films
    Dracula. Dir. Todd Browning. With Bela Lugosi. Universal Studios,
        1931.
c. Videocassettes or Filmstrips
    Hamlet. Videocassette. Dir. Laurence Olivier. With Olivier. Two
        Cities Films Ltd., 1948. 155 min. Based on William Shake-
        speare's Hamlet.

   d. Lectures and Speeches

Perkins, David. "Mrs. Gardner's Circle: T. S. Eliot." Isabella Stewart Gardner Museum. Boston, 2 Nov. 1989.

   e. Interviews

   1) *Interview conducted by the researcher*

Rubin, Arlene. Telephone interview. 24 May 1990.

   2) *Interview from a radio or television program*

Dove, John. "Training for the Boston Marathon for College Credit." All Things Considered. By David Wright. National Public Radio. WGBH, Boston, 15 Apr. 1991.

   f. Works of Art

   1) *Exhibited painting*

Monet, Claude. Rouen Cathedral Facade. Museum of Fine Arts, Boston.

   2) *Photograph of a painting*

Monet, Claude. La Cathédrale de Rouen. National Gallery of Art, Washington, DC. P. 174 in Monet. By Robert Gordon and Andrew Forge. New York: Abrams, 1984.

   g. On-line database or electronic index

   1) *Database*

Gan, V. "Portrait in the News: Richard Cheney." Current Digest of the Soviet Press 26 April 1989. Dialog file 645, accession #00024023.

   2) *Electronic index*

Paulsen, Alice. "Parents want to be sure racism is curbed." Green Bay Press-Gazette 23 May 1989. NewsBank Electronic Index, 1989. Soc. 36:A12.

   3) *Computer Software*

Polhemus, Neil. Statgraphics. Vers. 1.0. Computer software. STSC, Inc., 1985. IBM PC/XT/AT, 384KB, disk.

D. SPECIFIC DIRECTIVES FOR WRITING BIBLIOGRAPHY CARDS

1. If an article or book is unsigned, start the bibliography entry with the title. (*See 1.c.2*)

2. If a pamphlet does not appear at regular intervals, treat it like a book; however, treat a pamphlet published at regular intervals like a magazine.

3. a. For a magazine, put the inverted date (20 Mar. 1990) right after the title of the magazine, followed by a colon and the page numbers (10–15) ending with a period. Abbreviate all months except May, June, and July. (*See 1.e.2*)

   b. For a journal, give the volume number after the title, then the date in parentheses, followed by a colon and page numbers as above. (*See 1.e.3*)

4. If more than one city is given for a publisher, use the first one.
5. When dealing with republications:
    a. If a book has been revised, write the number of the edition you are using immediately after the title, ending with a period. Follow this sentence with the usual publication information. (*See 1.d.3*)
    b. If a book has been reprinted, give the original publication date, followed by a period, immediately after the title. Then give publication information for the work you are using. (*See 1.d.1*)
6. a. The formal bibliography and footnote entries for an encyclopedia article require only the author, title of article, title of encyclopedia, date and/or edition. For the bibliography card, also give the volume and page number which you will need for your footnotes. Note that many articles are signed only with initials which are identified elsewhere in the encyclopedia. (*see 1.c.1 & 1.c.2 and bibliography sample card for encyclopedia entry*)
    b. When using a dictionary as a source, follow the form for an encyclopedia entry. (*See 1.c.1 & 1.c.2 etc.*)
7. If there is more than one group responsible for a government document, put the larger group first, the smaller group second, etc. (*See f.1.b.*)
8. When making references to the Bible, cite the book of the Bible (abbreviated), chapter and verse, but never a page number (Ex: Gen. 1:16–20). Specify the version of the Bible used (Ex: King James, American Revised, etc.).
9. When using information from an on-line database or an electronic index, use the regular form for printed works, but add the name of the service and the identifying number, separated by a comma. (*See 2.g.1 & 2.g.2*)

IV

Making Card Notes

A. TAKING NOTES

Once you have established that there is a range of reliable and accessible information on your subject, you will begin to take notes. You will need 3 x 5 cards and a protective container for them. Alternatively, computer programs for notetaking exist and are increasingly useful; such programs allow the researcher to record and categorize data and to call it up again in the original categories or in cross-referenced categories. Whether one uses a computer or an index card system, however, one must learn the fundamental skill of setting up categories appropriate to the data.

As you read, note the facts, ideas, and opinions relevant to your topic on the cards or in your computer program. The notetaking stage of the paper is a very important one, for the accuracy with which you read and the discrimination you show in choosing data appropriate to support and develop your topic will determine the quality of the content of your final paper.

Enter a single piece of information on each card. Although this process may seem inefficient at this stage, it will facilitate the organization of your paper later. If you put just one item of information on each card, you will then have freedom to organize your material as your paper begins to develop. Because you will undoubtedly need to redefine and refocus your limited topic as your research progresses, the flexibility provided for reorganization by recording *one bit of data per card* is crucial.

Here is a model card followed by an explanation of it:

```
┌─────────────────────────────────────┐
│                                      │
│   Labor  of  monks—reduced   DB      │
│   ─────────────────────────  222     │
│   Servants in monasteries often      │
│   equaled, sometimes exceeded,       │
│   number of monks.                   │
│                                      │
│                                      │
│                                      │
└─────────────────────────────────────┘
```

1. At the upper right of each card be sure to include a code which identifies author (by initial of last name) and book (by initial of title) and the *page number* from which the information is taken. This information will be crucial for footnotes later on.

2. On the upper left of each note card, write a topical heading for the natural division of the subject under which the note falls. While it is not always possible to create headings early in the research process, and while you may not know the final divisions of your paper at first, be sure to create headings after you have written about twenty note cards. For an eight to ten-page paper, you will probably narrow down to ten or fewer final headings. For example, the writer of the student essay in Appendix A used the following categories to organize and identify the material for her paper: Fixed games in baseball before 1919; Comiskey, Charles; White Sox players; Landis, Judge Kennesaw; World Series 1919. If you are using a computer note-card system, remember to include similarly appropriate key words which will enable you to call up related data easily.

3. Once again, *make only one entry on each note card*. Write notes concisely; use fragments, full sentences, or direct quotations as seems appropriate.

4. *Use quotations marks* whenever you quote the exact words of a source even if you are recording just a phrase in the author's own words.

5. Do not number note cards. Their order will certainly change as you organize your paper.

6. Use only one side of each note card so that you can look over your note cards quickly and see the extent of information under each heading.

7. Write notes in ink because pencil fades.

B. CORRECT AND INCORRECT NOTE TAKING TECHNIQUES

I. Limiting information

Right:

<u>Labor of monks—limited</u>	CFI
	175
Monks did only writing, manuscript copying, and crafts.	

Wrong:

<u>Labor—St. Benedict</u>	BR
	85
St. Benedict said: work in fields is blessing for monks. Work in fields, cleaning, cooking done by hired servants. St. Benedict: "idleness is an enemy of the soul."	

Not even the heading of the second card is appropriately limited nor does it specify the relationship between the topic "Labor" and the man "St. Benedict." The material could be separated onto several note cards, two of which might be headed "<u>Labor: Attitude of St. Benedict.</u>" One card might say "St. Benedict calls work in the fields a blessing for monks" while the other card might read "St. Benedict states: 'Idleness is an enemy of the soul.'" Be sure to record material accurately. If the source made a cause/effect statement about the lack of hard labor by monks, the note needs to reflect that idea: for example, "Lack of hard labor by monks harmful to spiritual atmosphere of the monastery."

2. Choosing whether to quote or to paraphrase

When you take down factual information, direct quotation will rarely be necessary. The record of a date, a name, or a place can probably be stated simply in your own words. Summarizing an author's opinion on an issue is often another matter, however. Be sure to quote directly any words which show an author's distinctive attitude or point of view. In the following examples, note the rhetorical nature of the question as well as the satirical tone. John of Oyton must be quoted directly in order to preserve both.

Right:

Monastic gluttony	CFI
	392

John of Oyton's attitude
"Which, I ask, is the graver transgression in the matter of flesh-eating? That of the Black monks (Benedictines), who eat it openly, or of the White monks (Cistercians), who often eat it secretly to repletion? For both have the same Benedictine Rule."

Wrong:

Monastic gluttony	CFI
	392

John of Oyton, 14th century economist, wonders whether Black or White monks are worse for eating flesh since one group does it openly and the other secretly.

2. Deciding the number of note cards to use

There should be a proportionate number of note cards for each source. Twenty cards, for example, from five pages of one book and a mere ten more cards from four other sources might indicate a lack of balance in your research. If you discover more than one source corroborating an important statement, you might record the code identification and page reference for each corroborating source on the initial card. This procedure will enable you to demonstrate that a fact, idea, or conclusion is indeed part of common knowledge. Although the total number of cards may vary, for a final paper of approximately eight pages you will need a minimum of seventy-five cards from which to work.

C. AVOIDING PLAGIARISM

There are two kinds of plagiarism: claiming an author's ideas, including the organization, as your own and using his or her words without acknowledgment. Intentional plagiarism is deliberately dishonest; unintentional plagiarism, while not deliberately dishonest, is nevertheless blameworthy.

Unintentional plagiarism often occurs because of improper note taking. If you take verbatim any words from a source, be sure to copy them on your note card accurately, to enclose them in quotation marks, and to give the exact source. Follow this procedure in taking notes whether you copy a whole section, a sentence, or just a striking phrase or word. If you do not take notes carefully, you are likely to transfer the words from the note to the first draft and then to the final copy without remembering to give credit to the actual author. Unless you want an exact quotation for a specific reason (see IV B.2), the safest procedure is to take notes completely in your own words.

An original passage and examples of four types of plagiarism of it appear below:

Original passage

. . . Social futurism must cut even deeper. For technocrats suffer from more than econo-think and myopia; they suffer, too, from the virus of elitism. To capture control of change, we shall, therefore, require a final, even more radical break away from technocratic tradition: we shall need a revolution in the very way we formulate our social goals.

Rising novelty renders irrelevant the traditional goals of our chief institutions—state, church, corporation, army and university. Acceleration produces a faster turnover of goals, a greater transience of purpose. Diversity or fragmentation leads to a relentless multiplication of goals. Caught in the churning, goal-cluttered environment, we stagger future shocked, from crisis to crisis, pursuing a welter of conflicting and self-cancelling purposes.

Nowhere is this more starkly evident than in our pathetic attempts to govern our cities. New Yorkers, within a short span, have suffered a nightmarish succession of near disasters: a water shortage, a subway strike, racial violence in the schools, a student insurrection at Columbia University, a garbage strike, a housing shortage, a fuel oil strike, a breakdown of telephone service, a teacher walkout, a power blackout, to name just a few. In New York's City Hall, as in a thousand city halls all over the high-technology nations, technocrats dash, firebucket in fist,

from one conflagration to another without the least semblance
of a coherent plan or policy for the urban future.[1]

EXAMPLES OF PLAGIARISM

I. Word-for-word plagiarism

> Social futurism must cut even deeper. To avoid the virus of
> elitism and to capture control of change, we require a radical
> breakaway from technocratic tradition and a revolution in the
> way we formulate our social goals. Now we stagger, future
> shocked, from crisis to crisis, pursuing a welter of conflicting
> and self-cancelling purposes and in a thousand city halls all over
> the high-technology nations, technocrats dash, firebucket in fist,
> from one conflagration to another without the least semblance
> of a coherent plan or policy for the urban future.

This plagiarism might well be the result of having copied sentences from
Toffler onto note cards and then putting them together in the paragraph.
If the writer had enclosed all the copied text in quotation marks and had
identified the source in a footnote, he or she would not be liable to the
charge of plagiarism; however, a reader might feel justifiably that the
writer's personal contribution to the discussion was not very significant.

2. The mosaic

> We are faced with a serious crisis in the Twentieth-Century
> society and need to capture control of the change that surrounds
> us. We need a revolution in the way we formulate our social
> goals. Cities like New York (which has, in a short span, faced a
> nightmarish succession of near disasters ranging from racial
> violence to a power blackout) stagger from crisis to crisis without
> the least semblance of a plan or policy for their urban futures.

In the mosaic, phrases have been moved out of their original order and
arranged in new patterns. There is really no way to make this mosaic
legitimate, for to put every stolen phrase within quotation marks would
produce an almost unreadable, and quite worthless, text.

3. The apt term

In the following passage the writer has not been able to resist the appro-
priation of two striking terms—"the virus of elitism" and "churning,
goal-cluttered environment."

---

[1] Alvin Toffler, *Future Shock* (New York: Random House, Inc., 1970) 403. Quoted by
permission of Random House, Inc.

> The problems caused by rapid and perplexing change must be dealt with in our society. In solving these problems we must be aware that technocrats on whom we might wish to depend are often committed to rigid economic theories and, moreover, suffer from the virus of elitism. They too are caught in this churning, goal-cluttered environment and thus cannot lead us towards the revision of our social goals that we so desperately need.

A perfectly proper use of the terms would be:

> The problems caused by rapid and perplexing change must be dealt with in our society. In solving these problems we must be aware that technocrats on whom we might wish to depend are often committed to rigid economic theories, and, moreover, in Alvin Toffler's phrase, suffer from "the virus of elitism." They too are caught in what Toffler calls the "churning, goal-cluttered environment" and thus cannot lead us towards the revision of our social goals that we so desperately need.

Terms like "technocrat" and "social goals" are so common that they do not need attribution.

4. Plagiarism of the idea

Even the paragraph in Example 3 must be footnoted to give full information as to the source of ideas in the passage.

> Since one of the principles of an education is the development of intellectual honesty, it is obvious that plagiarism is a particularly serious offense and the punishment for it is commensurately severe. What a penalized student suffers can never really be known by anyone else; what the student who plagiarizes and "gets away with it" suffers is less public and probably less acute, but the corruptness of the act, the disloyalty and baseness it entails, must inevitably leave an ineradicable mark on the individual as well as on the institution of which he or she is privileged to be a member.[2]

---

[2] Much of the preceding material in IV.C except for the examples, is quoted from Harold C. Martin and Richard M. Ohmann, *The Logic and Rhetoric of Exposition.* Revised Edition. (New York: Holt, Rinehart and Winston, 1964) 275–278. Quoted by permission of Holt, Rinehart and Winston.

THE
WRITING
PROCESS

V

Planning the Paper

A. GETTING STARTED

Planning a paper is a creative process. You will need to work on your thesis statement and your outline concurrently. It is generally useful to begin with a tentative thesis statement.

B. WRITING A THESIS STATEMENT

A thesis is a one or two sentence statement which expresses the basic idea a paper will develop. Writing the thesis is a crucial step in the preparation of any paper because the thesis determines focus, length, and type of organization of the paper.

A GOOD THESIS IS RESTRICTED, PRECISE, AND UNIFIED.

I. Restriction

The thesis must indicate which of several approaches to the subject the writer will take. It thus limits the scope of the paper to what can be properly discussed in the space available. For example, such a thesis as "The Japanese Relocation Camps set up in the early 1940s had many effects on the people detained in them" is vague because it does not specify what particular effects the author will discuss.

Notice that the following thesis clearly states which effects will be discussed and thus restricts the writer to something that may be explained fairly thoroughly in 2500 words:

> The Japanese Relocation Camps set up in the early 1940s had the short-term effect of making the Japanese Americans intensify their patriotism to prove their loyalty to the United States and the long-term effect of breaking family traditions and causing poverty.

The unrestricted thesis gives the reader no real clue to what the author plans to write, and often makes the writer think the purpose is clear when he or she has little more than a general subject. An unrestricted thesis invites vague thinking, meandering organization, and superficiality.

2. Precision

A thesis should be phrased in words which permit only one interpretation. Especially, it should avoid words and phrases that are so general that they convey no exact meaning. "Organic gardening is an interesting hobby" or "Winston Churchill had a colorful career" are useless as thesis statements because the key words "interesting" and "colorful" could mean almost anything. If you intend to write "about" a subject, you have not yet established your purpose. You have merely lulled yourself into a false sense of achievement by the vagueness of your words. In a thesis, precise use of words is more important than effect.

3. Unity

To be unified, a thesis must commit the writer to investigate only one dominant idea. Such a thesis as "Hitler made serious tactical errors and refused to listen to his generals" requires the writer to do two things, not one. A paper with this double purpose will almost certainly fall into two parts having little connection with each other. "Because Hitler thought his generals were conspiring against him, he refused to heed their advice, causing him to make a series of major tactical errors" is a thesis that fuses the two parts into a unified purpose statement.
Another example:

Co-educational colleges have grown rapidly in America and fulfill a social need. (not unified)

Co-educational colleges have grown rapidly in America because they fulfill a social need. (unified)

Beware of the use of *and* in a thesis statement as a coordinating conjunction between two independent clauses, for *and* often signals that you have not carefully considered the relationships between your ideas. Other connectors that do provide a logical relationship between ideas are:

when, after, until, while	(time)
because, as, whereas, since	(explanation or cause)
in order that, so that, that	(purpose)
although, if, while, even though	(condition)
on the one hand . . . on the other	
hand, but, yet, however, nevertheless	(contrast)

consequently, therefore, as a result   (result)
not only . . . but also   (parallel addition)

4. The choice of the logical connectors in the thesis forecasts the organizational structure of the essay

If your essay is to be a comparison/contrast essay, you might select connectors such as *but, on the one hand . . . on the other hand.* If your essay is to be an analysis of the causes of an event, you might select the *because* or the *in order to* connectors. (Example: "Single-sex schools have become coeducational in order to attract a wider range of students as well as to bolster their flagging economies.")

If your essay will contain a section dealing with a condition that needs exploring and explaining in relation to the main idea, you might select an *although* connector. For example, "Although Mahler's innovations in symphonic form were ignored or misunderstood by the critics of his era, they are today recognized as one of his greatest achievements." Such an essay would focus primarily on the main clause but would also provide for an introductory section on Mahler's critics' ignoring what has come to be so highly regarded by modern-day critics. Similarly, such a thesis as "Although Charlotte Brontë wrote under a pseudonym, she was not afraid to tackle problems of women who were exploited by society" allows one to focus in on the main topic of Charlotte Brontë as social critic through an introductory discussion of how her use of a pseudonym reveals her to be the victim of a male-dominated society.

5. Two basic methods of organization

> *Rhetorical Induction*—the process of examining instances to find
> in them generalizations that are acceptable.
> *Rhetorical Deduction*—the process in which the writer begins
> with a generalization and through analysis of its parts and of
> specific examples verifies its truth.

Example of a paragraph organized inductively:

> If you do not mind having an aching back and dirty finger-
> nails; if you prefer a sunburnt neck and hands to an even tan; if
> you can spend Monday combatting potato bugs and aphids and
> return on Tuesday to make war against Japanese beetles; if you
> refuse to go to the beach on the hottest weekend of the year
> because the first tomato is due to ripen—you have the makings
> of a gardener in you. Of course you will soon become aware that
> your garden is both a millstone and an obsession, but all that
> will not matter the day you pick your first cool, green cucumber.
> When you eat the first green beans or zucchini or corn, back-

aches and bugs will be seen in their true perspective. *You will realize that gardening is a strenuous, frustrating but ultimately satisfying activity.*

Example of a paragraph organized deductively:

> *Birthday celebrations are joyous nightmares.* Fondly we remember that childhood birthday party, the multi-colored dripping popsicles, the sticky icing on our fingers, the blobs of wax from melting candles on the special party cloth. Happily we recall playing "pin-the-tail-on-the-donkey" and "musical chairs" and even the screams of anger when we did not win the prize. The day was *our* day; we were the center of attention and we still are at our adult birthday celebrations. There are still gifts and occasionally party hats and streamers. But the table cloth is white and neat now and the silver gleaming and the voices more subdued, and in the course of the "happy birthday" song we think of the passing of time and covertly watch the faces around us, wondering whether we too so obviously show our age. And then we know that we would gladly trade this polite and ordered celebration for the joyous "nightmare" of our childhood birthday party.

Notice the placement of the italicized topic sentence in each paragraph.

In a longer paper the thesis statement will naturally be more complex than the topic sentences of the above paragraphs:

> The childish stories she invented with her siblings, her attentive readings of Byron, and her intense love of the Yorkshire landscape all prepared Emily Brontë to write her masterpiece *Wuthering Heights*.

This thesis suggests a paper divided into three sections of approximately equal length. Notice that the order provides for an initial chronological approach and places the most general idea last. The reasoning in the paper will probably be inductive:

> Heathcliff in *Wuthering Heights* and Mr. Rochester in *Jane Eyre* are both examples of the Gothic hero, but Heathcliff is an amoral devil while Rochester is merely a slightly immoral man.

This thesis suggests a definition section followed by compare/contrast development. This working from a generalization to an examination of particular cases is deductive. While many writers prefer to place the thesis of an essay in the first paragraph and to work deductively, most topics can be handled by either method of organization.

C. MAKING THE OUTLINE

1. Indicate main section topics

When you know your subject thoroughly and have developed a tentative thesis statement, it is time to make a tentative outline for the paper. Read through all of your note cards and sort them into the major divisions which correspond to the major divisions of your thesis statement. There are usually three to five of these divisions. If your note cards do not correspond to the thesis statement, you must stop to revise your thesis *or* to collect more data. After you have sorted the cards into major divisions, write a section sentence for each of the major divisions. These main divisions usually are equal in importance. Also, the structure of the section sentences should be parallel. Arrange these main section sentences in a logical order and number them with Roman numerals. (I, II, etc.)

2. Indicate subsections or paragraph topics

Read through each major division of cards to discover subsections. Each subsection will be a paragraph in your essay. Create a topic sentence that corresponds to each subsection. Arrange these topic sentences in a logical order and number them with capital letters, preceded by the appropriate Roman numeral. (IA, IB, etc.) Although you will include many details in support of each paragraph topic sentence in your essay, you do not need to indicate these paragraph details in your outline. Be sure, however, that you have a sufficient number of cards providing details for each paragraph. If you discover your information to be inadequate, look up additional details.

3. The form of the outline

Keep the following points in mind:

a. Label your outline sections in the following way: Roman numerals for section sentences, capital letters for paragraph topic sentences. (Were you to include paragraph examples, they would be labeled with Arabic numerals; details of the examples would be labeled with lowercase letters.)

b. Each section sentence contains one part of the thesis statement. Each paragraph topic sentence presents one part of the section sentence.

c. Both section topics and paragraph subtopics *must* be expressed in full sentences to show completed ideas.

d. Each section must contain at least two paragraph subtopics. That is, if you have an *A*, you must have a *B*.

e. Keep your outline as simple as possible. Be sure that sections are equally important in content and roughly comparable in length.

f. *Be sure to write on one side of the sheet only* so that you can see the entire structure at a glance.

g. You must include your thesis statement at the top of your outline.

4. Sample outline

Thesis Statement: Although the institution of monasticism contributed greatly to medieval life through a distribution of charity and the atmosphere of learning and culture which surrounded it, the daily life of the individual monastery was often rendered corrupt by the frequent bypassing, both by the abbots and the monastic community in general, of the traditions and the way of life established by St. Benedict's Rule.

I. Medieval society benefited from the presence of the monasteries because of the charity and hospitality they distributed to the poor and travelers, and because of the many intellectual and cultural contributions they had to offer.

   A. According to monastic tradition, the monks offered charity by means of guesthouses and meals to the poor and to travelers, thus benefiting much of the population.

   B. The monasteries were also great centers for intellectual and cultural growth; the monks were among the most educated people in the world, and they initiated a great many of the important advances in literature, architecture, and music.

II. The abbot, the most important member of the monastic community, was gradually forced to relinquish his role as the father of the community; in order to fulfill his obligations as a feudal lord, he could no longer live as an ordinary monk nor set a good example to his fellow monks.

   A. As his monastery began to possess more and more land, and as his feudal and administrative responsibilities increased, the medieval abbot found himself to be increasingly estranged from the ordinary life of his abbey.

   B. Since the abbot was the very "pivot on which the life of the monastery turned," if he were a strong, spiritual man, the monastery would follow suit, but conversely, if he were either weak, or highly secular, the monks could do (and did) as they pleased.

III. The high ideals set forth in the monastic Rules were often rendered corrupt by not being followed word for word and were sometimes abandoned almost entirely.

   A. Since they followed the secular example set by the abbots, it was a common sight to see monks wandering through the medieval countryside, a direct affront to St. Benedict's Rule, which dictates strict confinement to the monastery.

   B. Ignoring the precept of poverty, which implies a complete renunciation of personal property, most medieval monks had possessions, ranging from costume jewelry to slaves, and varying amounts of money.

C. By tradition, and St. Benedict's Rule, butcher's meat was forbidden to the monks except under certain conditions such as sickness or meals with guests, and eating was, at all times, to be in moderation; in actuality, however, monks were commonly satirized as gluttons, and meat was a standard part of their diet.

D. In disregard of the old Benedictine principle *ora et labora,* pray and work, virtually all monks had ceased any heavy manual labor by the medieval period and were primarily idle.

E. The sexual immorality of the monks, while not universal, nor as widespread as some of the other corruptions mentioned above, still existed to a significant degree; the fact that it existed at all is disturbing.

5. Omit introduction and conclusion in the outline

Every completed essay must contain both an introduction and a conclusion, yet these labels should be omitted when you outline an essay. Only the logical structure and the factual content of an essay, not its stylistic devices, are included in the outline. (See further discussion of Introduction and Conclusion in Chapter VI B and C.)

VI

Writing the First Draft

A. USE OF NOTE CARDS AND OUTLINE TO DEVELOP THE FIRST DRAFT

You have gathered information while doing research and taking note cards, and you have thought through the logical structure of the paper while making the outline. The first draft is the step in which you fill in the outline. To write the first draft, all you need are your note cards and your outline; no books should be used.

Check over the ordering of note cards, which you sorted according to headings while planning the outline. Make sure (1) that each card is useful for its subsection, (2) that you are not keeping some cards because they are too interesting to set aside even if they are irrelevant, and (3) that you have enough information to develop each subsection fully.

The outline presents the order of ideas in your paper. Sentences for major sections in the outline (I, II, etc.) do not appear as topic sentences for separate paragraphs, but may be adapted for use as transitions. Each subsection heading (IA, IB, etc.) presents the main idea for one paragraph. Thus, IA is the main idea for the first paragraph after the introduction; IB is the main idea for the paragraph after that. Beside each paragraph in the first draft, write the number and letter of the subsection in the outline which it develops. Develop the main idea for each paragraph fully with facts and explanations. Unsubstantiated generalizations are not acceptable; solid, well-developed paragraphs will make your paper convincing.

B. THE INTRODUCTION

Because the introduction is the first paragraph (or paragraphs) in the paper, it must serve at least four functions. First, it should catch the reader's attention. A striking fact, a question, a provocative quotation, a brief anecdote are among the devices you might use to engage the reader's attention. Second, the introduction should indicate the subject of the paper. In a paper with a deductive structure, the introduction might state the central idea; in a paper with an inductive structure, it might pose the question which the paper will ultimately answer or delineate which area of the subject will be discussed. The third function of the introduction is to establish the tone of the paper—the attitude of the author toward subject and reader, and the level of formality. In most essays the tone will tend to be formal, but it should not be stiff. Finally, the introduction serves to give brief but necessary background information.

Were you writing your essay, for example, on Charlotte Brontë's struggle to become a novelist, you might introduce the subject with a brief anecdote of how Charlotte Brontë went to the publishing company, Smith, Elder & Co., that had accepted *Jane Eyre*. The publishers, expecting a man because she had written the novel under a male pseudonym, Currier Bell, were startled to see a small, rather dumpy female enter their office. You might follow this anecdote with questions: What caused Charlotte Brontë to assume a pseudonym? Did her unprepossessing size and use of a false name reveal timidity, or did they cloak and protect her aggressiveness? Such questions would prepare for an exploration of the cultural milieu in which Charlotte Brontë wrote. This anecdotal method will engage the reader's attention and establish necessary background information.

If you decide to begin with a quotation, you might proceed in the following manner: For an essay dealing with the Borgias' abuse of power, this quotation from Shakespeare, "Boundless intemperance/In nature is a tyranny. It hath been/The untimely emptying of the happy throne,/And fall of many kings." (*Macbeth*. IV. iii. 67–70.) serves to catch the reader's attention, to establish the theme of the essay, and to convey the attitude of the author toward the subject.

Because the thesis of the problem-centered essay in Appendix C is stated in its conclusion, the function of its introduction is, first, to establish a context, an overview, for all that follows. Second, it delineates the specific focus of the essay (see the last sentence of the introductory paragraph). And, third, it stimulates the reader's interest by indicating that a conventional view of the subject material is, in fact, incorrect.

The Age of Faith, The Golden Age of Monasticism—epithets that are commonly applied to the European Middle Ages. They evoke in our minds a time of great Christian feeling, a time when the lives of most people revolved around the Church, and when a person of deep religious convictions naturally gravitated toward life in a monastic community, living piously in prayer and holy labor. Not so, for most inhabitants of medieval monasteries were not the devout and devoted individuals we often consider them to be; many were younger sons of nobles, with family property entailed away from them by primogeniture, who had no choice but to enter a monastery. Others were noble bastards, whose fathers wished them out of the way at a minimum expense, or criminals, for whom the tonsure was an alternative to prison.[1] Consequently, the pious and holy ideals of monastic life were very often set aside, the monks seeming to be rather members of a "rich bachelor fraternity"[2] than the spiritual and self-denying men they were supposed to be. In spite of the general irreligious atmosphere and the many infractions of the monastic Rules, however, the overall influence of the many abbeys and priories was positive, for they provided the opportunity to learn and study in a society where intellectual knowledge was usually secondary (especially among the lower classes) to physical prowess. The monks were also the medieval equivalent of a welfare and hostel system: they distributed alms and food to the needy and poor, and the monastery guest house was the temporary home of many travelers. The façade of the monasteries of Medieval Europe is that of a solid institution that benefited society. A closer look, however, reveals the many corruptions with which it was riddled. The gradual decline from the grand monastic tradition of St. Benedict's Rule, the first and greatest of the monastic Rules, and the secularization which accompanied it were typical of medieval monachism.

For a two-paragraph introduction that employs a metaphor, defines a key term, and provides necessary background information, see the paper in Appendix B.

C. THE CONCLUSION

A paper reaches its *substantive* conclusion when it has answered the questions or resolved the problem initially stated. The substantive conclusion is thus part of the main content of the paper. The *stylistic* conclusion, on the other hand, is that which comes after the substantive conclusion and is thus in a position of emphasis. Although some papers will omit the stylistic conclusion, all papers must contain a substantive conclusion.

Because readers are likely to remember what the substantive conclusion says, be sure this last paragraph includes what you want them to retain. You might choose to include your thesis in the concluding paragraph, especially if your essay focused on a problem. For example, here is the conclusion of the student's paper on the World Series Scandal of 1919 cited in VI. B. and found in Appendix A:

Thus, because fixed games existed long before 1919, because team owner Charles Comiskey paid his players unfairly, and because some of the players who disapproved of the scheme, nevertheless, did not want to be excluded from it, eight members of the Chicago White Sox agreed to lose the World Series of 1919. This scandal threatened the future of baseball until 1921, when baseball's first commissioner, Judge Landis, imposed severe punishments on the eight players in an effort to convince angry fans that he was purifying the game. In a way, the scandal of 1919 was inevitable because of the prevalence of corruption and the weakness of baseball's officials. Fortunately, Landis became involved in the situation. Some people argue that Landis's punishments, particularly of Weaver and Jackson, were too harsh. But Landis was correct. Had he allowed Jackson and Weaver to continue playing, he probably would not have convinced fans that baseball was once again clean. Landis needed to prove that he would not allow any player even remotely associated with corruption to stay in the game. Landis also sent the message to other players that he would tolerate no further corruption. Thus, President Taft was correct in stating baseball was a "clean, straight, game." It never had been before, but because Landis intervened, he saved the game from self-destructing.

In writing a stylistic conclusion, you might restate the main point in an interesting and fresh way, or you might indicate the significance of what you have shown in the essay. The conclusion should also give your readers a sense of completion, of coming to an end. Reminding the readers of the opening paragraph by repetition of a key word, phrase, or idea will bring them to see how much they have learned since then. Oftentimes if you have begun with an anecdote, you might end by concluding it. For example, in the essay on Charlotte Brontë, the writer might conclude that the publishers, although dismayed at their first sight of Charlotte Brontë, found her not a prudish, provincial little woman, but a high-spirited, mordant critic of social institutions. A well-chosen quotation might also sum up the thrust of the paper. For example, here is the conclusion of a student's paper on Eugene Victor Debs:

So Eugene Victor Debs who began his fight for working class rights as a reformer became a revolutionary. As head of the American Railway Union, he wished to bring capital and labor closer together, but as a socialist he wished to overthrow the capitalist class. The capitalists themselves, in trying to subdue Debs, brought about this change. Capitalism thought it had destroyed Debs; it had merely made him. Debs's own statement is the best summary of this change. "I have tried the step-at-a-time policy, I have been an opportunist, but after years of experience and work and agitation, gentlemen, I have landed on a bedrock of socialism and from that I will not move."

D. ACKNOWLEDGMENT OF SOURCES

Much of any research paper is based on sources. Acknowledge these sources; that is, state in a footnote where you found a particular piece of data. The purposes of such acknowledgment are (1) to enable the reader to pursue an interesting idea or fact further, and (2) to give credit to the person whose work you have read. To claim someone else's work as your own is dishonest. To fail to give credit out of carelessness is both undisciplined and dishonest.

"But," you may say, "then everything in my paper will be footnoted." The organization, style, and conclusions will be your own, but you will, indeed, have many footnotes, for you should give the source for:

> a direct quotation
> an indirect quotation
> an opinion or conclusion not originally yours
> a statistic or result of a study
> a distinctive form of organization
> a fact not part of common knowledge

As a general rule, a fact is considered part of common knowledge if you have found it in three different sources: for example, that Benjamin Franklin's original trade was printing. A less well-known fact, such as the weight of the world's smallest mushroom, or a controversial fact, such as the wisdom of the bombing of Hiroshima, should be credited. If a whole paragraph in your paper is based on ideas from a source, put a footnote at the end of the paragraph indicating that source. As you gain more experience, you will develop surer judgment about when to credit sources, but remember the rule, *when in doubt, footnote.*

E. FOOTNOTES IN THE FIRST DRAFT

In the first draft put all footnotes in parentheses right after the material to be footnoted. Cite the code for author (first initial of last name) and title (first initial of title), and the page number. Here is an example based on the student paper in Appendix B:

> Primates show strength not only when two animals confront each other, but also when one animal acts alone, as in the famous chimpanzee "charging displays" where males swing huge branches, even small trees, in violent display of their dominance. (VI 28)

Do not number your footnotes, for their order may change as you revise sections of your paper.

F. EVEN MORE CONSIDERATIONS FOR THE FIRST DRAFT

1. Use only one side of each sheet of paper, and use every other or every third line. Also leave substantial margins on each side. These procedures will leave space for rewriting and editing.
2. Keep the different sections in proportion to each other, not too much space devoted to one section and too little to another.
3. Use the third person and an objective style throughout. Avoid all use of *I* or *me* or *my* or *you*. Leave yourself out of the paper.
4. Avoid the passive voice; not "This was said by Kennedy . . . ," but "Kennedy in the first debate with Nixon said that. . . ."
5. You must key your paper to your outline. To show what part of the outline each paragraph develops, immediately before each paragraph put a Roman numeral to indicate the section and a capital letter to indicate the subsection, e.g., I.A.

G. PROOFREADING AND REVISING THE FIRST DRAFT

Once you have written a complete first draft, you should go through it critically and revise it in order to make it as strong as possible. Writing is a craft and takes much deliberate effort. This means that before handing the paper in to the teacher, you may have to rewrite a large part of the draft or revise some parts a number of times. You should add, eliminate, or rearrange material where appropriate. You will probably have to rewrite and edit sentences, paragraphs, or even whole sections. Sometimes you may decide to move a section to an entirely different place in the essay. Make your revisions clearly, fully, and legibly so that the teacher can understand easily what you have written and so that you will remember what you meant when you are writing the final draft.

You should consider the following points when revising. Go over the list, note areas in which you tend to be weak, and then check through your first draft, looking especially for those trouble spots.

Paragraphs:

1. Is there a single paragraph for each subtopic in the outline?
2. Is each paragraph clearly and logically organized?
3. Does all the material in the paragraph relate to the topic sentence?
4. Excluding the paragraphs of introduction and conclusion, does the first draft have the same number of paragraphs as there are capital letters in the outline?

Development:

1. Are specific facts, details, and examples used in order to avoid unsubstantiated generalizing?
2. Has the significance of the evidence been explained?
3. Does each section present both an adequate and a concise treatment of its subject?

Grammar and Mechanics:

1. Check your work for errors of grammar. Are there problems of subject-verb agreement, dangling or misplaced modifiers, faulty parallelism, incorrect or vague reference, faulty subordination, inaccurate comparisons, incorrect pronoun reference or case? You should obtain and use a grammar handbook.
2. Check your work for errors in word choice and usage. Have you confused words such as affect-effect or imply-infer?
3. Check your work for punctuation errors. Are there any run-on sentences, comma splices, or fragments? Have you used quotation marks, commas, and semicolons accurately? Here is another instance in which a grammar handbook is invaluable.
4. Check your spelling. Have you availed yourself of a dictionary, an electronic spell-checker, or a word processing spell-check program?

Style:

1. Are the introduction and conclusion strong and interesting?
2. Is the style appropriately objective and consistent throughout? Does it avoid slang, colloquialisms, contractions, and reference to self?
3. Are sentences varied in pattern and length?
4. Is the writing concise? Could material be combined and relationships indicated by coordination or subordination? Could some materials or wordiness be struck out?
5. Are there valid transitions from one point to another within paragraphs, from one paragraph to another, from one main division to another? (See Section VII A for an example of a weak and an improved Transition.)
6. Are sources acknowledged when appropriate?

H. SUBMITTING THE FIRST DRAFT TO THE TEACHER

With the first draft, submit a copy of the final thesis statement and outline as approved by the teacher. You may have found that as you wrote the first draft, you needed to make some changes in the order of your paper. Revise the outline so it agrees with the paper, and submit this revised outline with your paper also.

VII

Preparing the Final Draft

A. REVISION OF THE FIRST DRAFT

While the teacher or instructor will read the entire first draft of your paper, he or she will comment in detail only on one or two sections and on the introduction and conclusion. This procedure requires you to apply criticism independently to the uncorrected sections of your paper. Before you begin to write the final draft, read through the entire paper carefully; identify and categorize mistakes and weaknesses in grammar, rhetoric, and style that have been indicated by the instructor. Then correct and revise one section at a time, being careful to look for identified weaknesses in the uncorrected sections. Make all necessary corrections and revisions on the first draft before preparing the final copy.

The following paragraphs come from the promising first draft of a student essay on whether apes have the ability to learn language as humans do. Although the student researched her subject thoroughly, she has created a kind of "wastebasket paragraph"; that is, she begins with a topic sentence (underlined) and tosses in related ideas from her notecards without explaining clearly the significance of the material. The teacher points out that the student needs to make her point more directly and to improve the connections between ideas.

> . . . Until the apes begin to converse appropriately as children do, most experts will not consider their signing *more of a* *transition* *needed here →* to be a form of human language.
>
> (III B) The apes created sign combinations that varied in order and that never increased in complexity, dem- onstrating the"lack of a child's ability to learn to make *clarify unclear* *reference* *the whenever* *it occurs.* more complicated utterances and, even more signifi- cantly, the lack of a child's sense of language's struc- ture. In human language, a sentence represents a com- plete idea through a group of words that have specific grammatical relations. These relations, unlike the words themselves, cannot be learned individually; they

constitute a part of the *grammar* of the language. (Psy-cholinguists) and linguists are in general agreement that the use of a human language indicates the knowledge of a grammar, even though a good deal of this knowledge is below the conscious level. (BC 891) The knowledge of a grammar that children naturally acquire explains their "ultimate ability to create an indeterminable number of meaningful sentences from a finite number of words." (PC 441) While a child may progress from "Mommy milk" to "Mommy, please give me some milk," the apes never moved to this more sophisticated level of expression; (TN 20) most longer utterances simply contained repeated signs. (GA 299) According to the reports of the Gardners and Patterson, the signs in the apes' sequences occured in all possible orders; (BC 893) therefore, there is no reason to believe that the apes are acting in accordance with a sense of sign order. Although word order in sign language is less of a "grammatical device" (TN 12) than in spoken language, it is still critical in distinguishing between utterances like "tickle me" and "me tickle" (TN 12–13) and therefore an important key to having a true grasp of the language. As stated by Duane Rumbaugh, a researcher at Georgia State University doing similar work to Terrace's "There is no solid evidence . . . that would indicate that the ape is capable of uing language with competence." (LA 57) According to many scientists, an apparent inability to use a language's structure denotes an inability to use language itself. Some, like Noam Chomsky, have particularly strong views: "It's about as likely that an ape will prove to have a language ability as that there is an island somewhere with a species of flightless birds waiting for human beings to teach them to fly." (AT 57) As another scientist has expressed it, "the skeptics raise the possibility that the apes have been making monkeys out of their human mentors." (AT 50)

Marginal annotations:
- Redundant ???
- Perhaps here there should be a compare/contrast comment focusing on the ape's inability to grasp language?
- Isn't this a new point demanding a bit more transition?
- sp
- Do avoid passive constructions wherever they occur.
- weak: Aren't you using this QT as a summary? Your lead-in to QT deemphasizes its importance.
- x typo
- Is that good? Bad? I can't tell.
- I'm left at P's end not esp. clear about what conclusion you want me to draw.
- vague
- Again I have trouble figuring out from this sentence the point-of-view you want to push me as a reader toward. Your neutrality (in language) becomes positively confusing here.
- It's not clear whether the QT comes from "some" or from Chomsky.

In reworking the above paragraph, the student went beyond a "fix-it" approach to think out how best to solve the logical issues commented on by the teacher. The following revision demonstrates that the student rethought organization and word choice and therefore succeeded in making the material her own.

REVISED III B

Not only did the apes fail to sense the conversational nature of language but, even more importantly, they also seemed to lack any sense of its structure. In natural language, a sentence represents a complete idea through a group of words that have specific grammatical relationships. The relations, unlike the words themselves, cannot be learned individually; they constitute a part of the *grammar* of the language. Linguists generally agree that the use of a human language depends upon the knowledge of its grammar, even though much of the knowledge is below the conscious level. (BC 891) The knowledge of a grammar that children naturally acquire explains their "ultimate ability to create an indeterminable number of meaningful sentences from a finite number of words"; (PC 441) that is, grammatical knowledge matures with the child, allowing him to progress from the simple imitation of phrases to the construction of sentences he has never heard before. <u>The apes</u>, on the other hand, <u>created sign combinations that varied in order and never increased in complexity, demonstrating their lack of the child's ability to learn to form more complicated utterances and, even more significantly, their lack of the child's sense of language's structure.</u> While a child may progress from "Mommy milk" to "Mommy, please give me some milk," the apes never advanced to this more sophisticated level of expression; (TN 20) most long utterances simply contained repeated signs. (GA 299) Furthermore, according to the reports of the Gardners and Patterson, the signs in the apes' sequences occurred randomly in utterances like "tickle me" and "me tickle." (TN 12–13) Given this apparent lack of a sense of linguistic order, as well as that of conversational ability and structural complexity, "(t)here is no solid evidence . . . that would indicate that the ape is capable of using (language) with competence." (LA 57)

An extraordinary revision - you go beyond my suggestions to clarify the paragraph's point-of-view and focus. It's so much more clearly expressed than the original; its logic (order of material) now works beautifully. You've solved all of the problems I saw in the first paragraph as well as ones I hadn't picked up on: that's <u>real</u> revising! Your judgement about what to edit/rework is excellent.

B. DETAILS OF MANUSCRIPT FORM

You have worked hard researching and writing a coherent essay about your subject; therefore, the appearance of your final copy warrants careful attention. Not only should you produce a neatly typed or handwritten

paper, but you should also take care to follow details of correct manuscript form, in particular the following items.

I. Title page

Give your paper an interesting title neither too general nor too cryptic.
Remember, it should describe the contents of the paper. Center the title
about four inches from the top of the paper. In the lower right quarter of
the page, indicate your name, the name of the typist if other than yourself, your class, the course title (or titles if the paper was an inter-
disciplinary project), and the date submitted, thus:

Jane M. Harding
Typist: Janet Smith
Expository Writing
United States History
May 27, 1991

Jon C. Kim
Senior English
May 31, 1991

2. Outline

Insert the outline immediately after the title page of the finished paper;
head it *Contents*. Do not number the pages on which the outline appears.

3. Body of the paper

Leave a margin of one and one-quarter inches at the left and one inch at
the right, at the top and at the bottom. Double-space the text and number
the pages at the top right in Arabic numerals beginning with page two of
the text. Indent quoted passages of more than three lines about an inch
from the margin of the text on both left and right, and do not use quotation marks; single-space the indented quotations.

   You may place footnotes at the bottom of the page or on a separate
sheet at the end of the paper, preceding the bibliography. Most word
processing programs allow the writer to place footnotes at the bottom of
the page and automatically make the necessary page format adjust-
ments. Note, however, that proper form requires that you single-space
footnotes of more than one line, and double-space between footnotes. The
citation number should be set in superscript. The first line of the footnote
should be indented five spaces. All lines after the first in each note must
begin at the margin.

4. Footnotes

The following are samples of footnotes which correspond to bibliography
entries in Section III C:

1. Printed Works

a. Single Works

Book by one author

¹ Fred J. Cook, Maverick: Fifty Years of Investigative Reporting (New York: G. P. Putnam's Sons, 1984) 138.

Another book by the same author

² Fred J. Cook, The Ku Klux Klan: America's Recurring Nightmare (Englewood Cliffs, NJ: J. Messner, 1980) 41.

Book by two authors

³ Sean Manley and Susan Belcher, O, Those Extraordinary Women! (Philadelphia: Chilton Book Company, 1972) 235.

Book by three or more authors

⁴ William L. Masterton et al., Chemical Principles (Philadelphia: Chilton Co., 1972) 372.

Edited work of one author

⁵ D. H. Lawrence, Complete Poems, eds. Vivian de Sola Pinto and F. Warren Roberts (New York: Viking Press, 1971) 19.

Translation

⁶ Julio Cortazar, Around the Day in Eighty Worlds, trans. Thomas Christensen (San Francisco: North Point Press, 1986) 79.

Corporate author

⁷ American Medical Association, The American Medical Association's Handbook of First Aid and Emergency Care (New York: Random House, 1980) 82.

Conference proceedings

⁸ Proceedings of the 1985 State Fish and Wildlife Directors Conference. 4–6 June 1985 (Washington, DC: U.S. Department of Commerce, National Marine Fisheries Service, 1986) 72.

Occasional report

⁹ Everett Mendelsohn, A Human Reconstruction of Science, a report prepared for a conference on women (Cambridge, MA: Radcliffe Institute, Apr. 1972) 2.

b. Collections

Previously published work in a collection

¹⁰ Paula Fox, "News from the World," Confrontation (Spring, 1975): 78–81, rpt. in Short Shorts: An Anthology of the Shortest Stories (Boston: David R. Godine, 1982) 242.

Work in an edited collection

¹¹ George Liska, "War and Order," Globalism and Its Critics, ed. William Taubman (Lexington, MA: D. C. Heath and Co., 1973) 42.

Edited collection from which two or more works have been cited

¹² Robert H. Williams, ed., To Live and To Die: When, Why and How (New York: Springer-Verlag, 1973) 24.

One work cited from previously cited edited collection

¹³ Gilbert S. Omenn, "Genetic Engineering: Present and Future," in Williams 51.

c. Encyclopedias
Signed article in an encyclopedia
[14] Esmond Wright, "Washington, George," Collier's Encyclopedia 1987 ed.
Unsigned article in an encyclopedia
[15] "Icarus," Encyclopedia Americana 1989 ed.
d. Revisions and Republications
Reprint or facsimile of an earlier edition
[16] Mary Elizabeth Braddon, Lady Audley's Secret (1887; New York: Dover, 1974) 93.
Reprint with new foreword, afterword, or introduction
[17] Clifton Fadiman, afterword, The Red Badge of Courage, by Stephen Crane (New York: Macmillan, 1967) 117.
Edition other than the first
[18] Lawrence Baum, The Supreme Court, 3rd ed. (Washington, DC: Congressional Quarterly, Inc., 1989) 53.
e. Magazines, Journals, and Newspapers
Signed magazine article
[19] Cait Murphy, "Hong Kong: A Culture of Emigration," The Atlantic Apr. 1991: 24.
Unsigned magazine article
[20] "Presidential Commission Cites Improvements in European Airport and Airway Safety," Aviation Week 26 Feb. 1990: 31.
Journal article
[21] Edward Mendelson, "Word Processing: A Guide for the Perplexed," Yale Review 74 (1985): 615.
Unsigned newspaper article showing edition
[22] "Alaska Oil by Land and Sea," New York Times 17 July 1977, nat'l ed.: A4.
f. Government Documents
Printed by Government Printing Office
Report by a government department
[23] United States Bureau of Labor Statistics, A Brief History of the American Labor Movement, 1970 ed. (Washington, DC: GPO, 1970) 120.
Report of hearings
[24] United States, Congress, Senate, Committee on Government Operations, Subcommittee on Intergovernmental Relations, and Committee on the Judiciary, Subcommittees on Separation of Powers and on Administrative Practice and Procedure, Hearings, 93rd Congress, 1st sess., vol. 1 (Washington, DC: GPO, 1973) 440.
Printed by a private publisher
[25] United States National Advisory Commission on Civil Disorders, Report of the National Advisory Commission on Civil Disorders, York Times Edition (New York: E. P. Dutton, 1968) 359.

g. Reviews
Book, exhibit or performance
[26] Tom Buckley, "Anyone for War?" rev. of <u>The Long Gray Line</u> by Rick Atkinson, <u>The New York Times Book Review</u> 22 Oct. 1989: 18.
h. Indirect Sources
[27] Marvin Schegel, <u>Ruler of the Reading: The Life of Franklin B. Gowan</u> (Harrisburg: Archives Publishing Co. of Pennsylvania, 1947) 72 as qtd. in Broehl 206.

2. Other Media
a. Television or Radio Programs
[28] <u>Private Lives, Public Trust</u> writ. Stephen Schlow, dir. Dimitri Miades, prod. WHDH (a CBS affiliate), Boston, 27 June 1990.
b. Films
[29] <u>Dracula,</u>dir. Todd Browning, with Bela Lugosi, Universal Studios, 1931.
c. Videocassettes or Filmstrips
[30] <u>Hamlet,</u> videocassette, Two Cities Film Ltd., 1948 (155 min.).
d. Lectures and Speeches
[31] David Perkins, "Mrs. Gardner's Circle: T. S. Eliot," Isabella Stewart Gardner Museum, Boston, 2 Nov. 1989.
e. Interviews
Interview conducted by the writer of the paper
[32] Arlene Rubin, Librarian, The Winsor School, telephone interview, 24 May 1990.
Interview from a radio or television program
[33] John Dove, "Training for the Boston Marathon for College Credit," <u>All Things Considered,</u> by David Wright, National Public Radio, WGBH, Boston, 15 Apr. 1991.
f. Works of Art
Exhibited painting
[34] Claude Monet, <u>Rouen Cathedral Facade,</u> Museum of Fine Arts, Boston.
Photograph of a painting
[35] Claude Monet, <u>La Cathédrale de Rouen,</u> National Gallery of Art, Washington, p. 174 in <u>Monet</u> by Robert Gordon and Andrew Forge (New York: Abrams, 1984).
g. Online Database or Electronic Index
Database or Electronic index
[36] V. Gan, "Portrait in the News: Richard Cheney," <u>Current Digest of the Soviet Press</u> 26 Apr. 1989: 2 (Dialog file 645, accession #00024023).
Computer software
[37] Neil Polhemus, <u>Statgraphics,</u> vers.1.0., computer software, STSC, Inc., 1985.

Additional Footnote Information:

a. In every case, be sure that the work to which you refer in a footnote is included in your bibliography.

b. The second time you cite a book, state the author but not the title of the work unless you are using two books by the same author, in which case you must give a brief title also.

c. Be aware that footnote punctuation differs from that in a bibliography entry.

d. Throughout the paper, number footnotes consecutively using Arabic numerals not followed by periods, parenthesis, or other marks. Put footnote numbers after punctuation at the end of the quotation or other material which requires acknowledgment. Put numbers above line of type both in the text and at the bottom of the page or on a separate sheet at the end of the paper.

e. You may use the following abbreviations and terms in footnote and bibliography entries:

ed.	editor	sc.	scene
eds.	editors	sec.	section
l.	line	trans.	translator
ll.	lines	vol.	volume
n.d.	no data (any missing publication information.)	vols.	volumes

f. *Ibid,* meaning "in the same place," and *op cit,* meaning "work already cited," are Latin forms that used to be common. They are not used by contemporary researchers although you may encounter them in your reading.

g. Below are sample footnotes for various situations:

First citation of a book (complete)[1]
Same work, different page[2]
First citation of a magazine article[3]
First citation of another book by an author previously cited[4]
Same author, different book previously cited (indicate which book)[5]
Author previously referred to but not immediately before this footnote[6]

[1]Zora Neale Hurston, Dust Tracks on a Road (Philadelphia: J. B. Lippincott Company, 1942) 75.
[2]Hurston 122.
[3]David Joselit, "Public Art & The Public Purse," Art in America July 1990: 145.

[4]Zora Neale Hurston, Their Eyes Were Watching God (Philadelphia: J. B. Lippincott Company, 1937) 87.
[5]Hurston, Dust Tracks 44.
[6]Joselit 143.

h. The authors have chosen this form of footnoting, an alternative sanctioned by the third edition of *The MLA Handbook;* the authors have not chosen the more radically revised form offered there which interrupts sentences in the text with bibliographical information. There are also other alternative forms of footnoting used in some specialized fields. Ask your teacher or consult *The MLA Handbook* for these other forms and for the names of other style manuals. What is crucial is to choose a clear form of footnoting and to *use it consistently.*

5. Bibliography

Include in the final bibliography only those sources from which you obtained usable material. Refer to section III C for models of correct form and content of entries. Do not number items in the bibliography. Arrange them alphabetically by author (or by title, if a work is unsigned). Do not indent the first line of a bibliography entry, but do indent subsequent lines, if any. Single-space each entry, but double-space between entries. Do not number the bibliography page.

6. Appendix (if necessary)

The appendix is the appropriate place for illustrative or explanatory material which you cannot incorporate into the text. The appendix should have a heading; do not number the pages in the appendix. Place the appendix between the footnotes (if you have used a separate sheet for them) and the bibliography.

7. Proofreading

As a final step in preparing the research paper, proofread thoroughly and make corrections carefully. Be sure to check for the most common errors: spelling, punctuation, capitalization, inadvertent omissions, and typographical mistakes. Reading the paper aloud will slow down reading speed, thereby enabling you to detect errors more readily. *Proofread your paper more than once;* make corrections neatly.

8. Submitting the Final Paper

Bind the paper neatly in a cover.

APPENDIX A

Field of Greed:
The World Series Scandal of 1919

Susan Pitts
Expository Writing
December 12, 1990

CONTENTS

Thesis Statement: Because fixed games existed long before 1919, because team owner Charles Comiskey paid his players unfairly, and because some of the players who disapproved of the scheme nevertheless did not want to be excluded from the fix, eight members of the Chicago White Sox agreed to lose the World Series of 1919, creating a scandal which threatened the future of baseball until 1921, when baseball's first commissioner, Judge Kenesaw Landis, imposed severe punishments on the eight players in order to convince angry fans that he was purifying the game.

   I. Although team owners and baseball officials realized that gambling and fixed games existed long before 1919, they almost always suppressed any investigations into fixed games because proving them was very difficult and because owners and officials knew that fans would not pay to see games they suspected were fixed; because of this unstated policy by owners and officials, many of the participants in the 1919 Series fix believed that, if found out, they would receive little or no punishment.

     A. Even before the Civil War, betting on baseball games was popular, and by the late 1800s, gamblers were bribing players into throwing games.

     B. Hal Chase, a first baseman for the Cincinnati Reds, exemplifies baseball's corruption in the years just prior to the 1919 series.

     C. Because baseball officials and owners did not want the public to discover baseball's corruption, they suppressed any investigations into fixed games; this unstated policy led many of the participants in the 1919 Series fix to believe that they would receive little or no punishment if found out.

  II. Although during the few years before the scandal the White Sox drew the largest crowds in all of baseball, team owner Charles Comiskey paid his players the lowest salaries and ignored any attempts by the players to improve their salaries; this cheapness provoked bitterness and resentment among his team members.

     A. Although the White Sox drew the largest crowds in all of baseball from 1917 to 1919, team owner Charles Comiskey paid his players the lowest salaries and was exceedingly cheap concerning team expenses and bonuses.

     B. Although the players often tried to negotiate higher salaries in their contracts, to which they were bound, Comiskey ignored their requests; furthermore, since Comiskey appeared to the fans to be a generous man, the White Sox could not air their grievances successfully in public.

  III. While greed caused four of the participants to lose the World Series, the other four participants disapproved of the plan, but because they were told the fix would proceed without them, they decided they did not want to be excluded from the money promised.

    A. First baseman Chick Gangil and shortshop "Swede" Risberg thought up the fix to earn money, and, along with pitcher Ed Cicotte and utility infielder Fred McMullin, proposed it to eager gamblers.

    B. These four conspirators coaxed the other four participants— Buck Weaver, Joe Jackson, Lefty Williams, and Happy Felsch— into losing the World Series by telling them the fix would happen with or without them.

IV. After the public discovered the fixing of the 1919 World Series, fans' distrust of players and their reluctance to go to games greatly diminished baseball's popularity until 1921, when baseball's first commissioner, Judge Kenesaw Landis, imposed severe punishments on the eight players in order to convince the public that he was purifying the game.

    A. Baseball fans' dismay at the fixing of the 1919 World Series and their new reluctance to go see games decreased baseball's popularity and threatened its future.

    B. In 1921, though a jury acquitted the eight players of conspiracy, the first commissioner of baseball, Judge Kenesaw Landis, after promising to rid baseball of corruption, prohibited the players from playing professional baseball again.

In 1910, President William Howard Taft proclaimed, "The game of baseball . . . is a clean, straight game, and it summons to its presence anybody who enjoys clean, straight athletics."[1] Such was not the case in 1919, however, when eight members of the Chicago White Sox conspired to throw the World Series. The players agreed with prominent gamblers to lose the series for $10,000 each; however, though they succeeded in losing the series, the players never received all of the money promised to them in the fix. Ironically, though rumors had abounded during the series that there was a fix, it was not until September of 1920, a full year later, that the public discovered the rumors were true—a Chicago grand jury which had been investigating gambling in baseball handed down indictments against the eight members of the White Sox. The public was shocked, but what they did not realize at the time was that the Black Sox, as they were dubbed during the scandal, were not the only players involved in corruption, nor were they the first.

Corruption in baseball existed even in its early years. Before the Civil War, betting on baseball games was popular, and by the late 1800s gamblers were bribing players into throwing games. In the early 1800s upper-class men played baseball in private clubs and many who watched the games, as well as many who played, betted on the games.[2] Baseball was an unorganized sport at this time, and the betting which occurred was minor. In the late 1800s, however, baseball became a fully organized sport, open to all classes, and gambling became more popular and more serious as professional gamblers became involved. Winning a bet was so important to professional gamblers that they often attempted physically to prevent players from making key plays—a gambler might throw stones at an outfielder trying to catch a crucial fly ball, or he might set off his gun to startle the player.[3] With the increasing popularity of gambling came the fixed game. To secure a successful bet, gamblers realized they could bribe players into losing games with money, whiskey, or women—some gamblers even threatened blackmail or violence.[4] Not all ballplayers were willing to cooperate with the gamblers, however; therefore, gamblers targetted with their bribes older players (near the end of their careers), poorly paid players, and players with personal problems.[5] Sometimes, though, gamblers could bribe whole teams into throwing games. In the 1860s, the Troy (New York) Haymakers were notorious for throwing games.[6] One might think fixed games would decrease baseball's popularity, but teams who fixed games took turns losing to each other so they would not arouse public suspicion.[7] Thus, even in its early years, gambling and fixed games were prevalent in baseball.

Hal Chase, a first baseman for the Cincinnati Reds, exemplifies baseball's corruption in the years just prior to the 1919 World Series. Chase was an excellent fielder and hitter who often arranged with gamblers to fix games. For years, Chase had the ability to throw games without arousing suspicion. If a batter hit a key ground ball to him, Chase would stop it correctly, but then he would throw the ball to first base just before the pitcher could catch it. Thus, the pitcher looked bad, and no one suspected Chase of throwing the game.[8] During a game in 1917, Chase attempted to bribe a relief pitcher into losing a tied game. The pitcher refused but lost the game anyway and Chase, thinking the pitcher lost purposely, gave him fifty dollars. The pitcher told his manager, who informed the National League President. A hearing was held for Chase, but he was acquitted because of insufficient evidence. Though Chase's manager, an honest man, refused to let Chase stay on his team, the New York Giants signed him, and Chase remained in baseball and continued to throw games. Though Chase exemplifies the corruption of players, he is proof of the deviation of team owners as well.

Because officials and team owners did not want the public to discover baseball's corruption, they suppressed any investigations into fixed games; this unstated policy led many of the participants in the 1919 Series fix to believe they would receive little or no punishment if found out. Team owners realized that satisfactory attendance at their games depended on the belief the games were completely honest; therefore, owners denied the existence of betting on baseball and had never punished any corrupt players prior to 1919.[9] It is possible that the players involved in the 1919 Series scandal did not believe team owners would punish them for their actions either.[10] Such beliefs may have stemmed from the Hal Chase incident. In 1920, journalist Hugh Fullerton wrote:

> The Chase case gave many players the idea they could play dishonestly and not be discovered . . . the club owners have always adhered to the policy of secrecy and have whitewashed every scandal and charge of crooked work on the grounds that it was for the good of the game. Their policy encouraged crooked ball players.[11]

Ed Cicotte, one of the White Sox fix participants, said during the trial that he assumed owners would protect him from punishment because he had seen how they protected other corrupt players in the past.[12] Thus, owners' attitudes influenced the White Sox in agreeing to lose the World Series.

Charles Comiskey was an owner whose attitudes about money seemed designed to foster corruption on his team. Although the White Sox drew the largest crowds in all baseball from 1917 to 1919, team owner Charles Comiskey paid his players the lowest salaries and was exceedingly cheap about team expenses and bonuses. Comiskey paid $65,000 to buy Joe Jackson from Cleveland, yet Jackson's salary with the White Sox was only $6,000 per year.[13] Jackson, one of the best players in baseball at this time, was the highest-paid player on the White Sox; however, the highest salary on the Cincinnati Reds team was $10,000 per year, the second highest $9,000, and the third highest $8,000.[14] In comparison with their achievements on the field, the Sox salaries were extremely low. Ed Cicotte was a fourteen-year veteran pitcher in 1919. He won twenty-eight games in 1917, (in comparison, 1990's highest game-winning pitcher won twenty-four games) but in 1919 received less than $6,000 per year.[15] During the 1919 season Comiskey promised Cicotte a $10,000 bonus if he won thirty games, but after Cicotte won twenty-nine games, Comiskey refused to let him pitch until the playoffs (when winning games is no longer included in a pitcher's record). Comiskey also promised the whole team a bonus if they won the 1917 pennant. When they did, their bonus was a case of champagne.[16] Comiskey was parsimonious in other areas, too. He gave his players a $3 per day meal allowance; all other teams received a minimum of $4 per day.[17] What did Comiskey do with all of his money? In 1909, Comiskey spent $500,000 rebuilding his ballpark.[18] Not only did he dedicate this park to the people of Chicago, but he also let them use the park for special events—for free.[19] Thus, to the public, Comiskey seemed a generous person.

Although the players often tried to negotiate higher salaries in their contracts, to which they were bound, Comiskey ignored their requests; furthermore, since Comiskey appeared to the fans to be a generous person, the White Sox could not air their grievances successfully in public. One of the White Sox's problems was the Reserve Clause, found in every major league player's contract. The clause stated that if a player refused to accept the terms offered to him by the owner, no other club could hire him.[20] Thus, a player could not really negotiate a salary at all—he either accepted the money offered him by the owner, or he did not play for that year. In 1918, Comiskey once again refused to discuss salary changes, and the White Sox threatened to strike.[21] In order to prevent controversy, however, their manager, "Kid" Gleason dissuaded them even though he agreed with his team's reasons for wanting to strike.[22] The White Sox could not complain openly about Comiskey, for who would believe Comiskey was cheap when he had recently dedicated his new ballpark to the people of Chicago? Thus, the White Sox, the most talented team in baseball, played year after year for the stingiest man in baseball, until the World Series scandal of 1919.

In spite of gamblers' history of bribing players, it was the players themselves who first proposed the fix to the gamblers. First baseman Chick Gandil and shortstop "Swede" Risberg thought up the plan to earn money, and, along with pitcher Ed Cicotte and utility infielder Fred McMullin, proposed it to eager gamblers. During the trial Ed Cicotte stated, "Before Gandil became a ball player, he was mixed up with gamblers . . . . That's where he got the idea to put the fix on the World Series."[23] Long after the trial, Gandil himself admitted it was he who was the first to approach gamblers with his plan.[24] Gandil discussed his idea with Risberg, and the two decided they needed eight players to agree to throw the series. McMullin overheard the discussion and wanted to be included.[25] Gandil then proposed the fix to Cicotte, who refused but later agreed. "I was thinking of my wife and kids and how I needed the money," he later stated in his confession.[26] Indeed, Cicotte needed the money to pay off a large mortgage on his Michigan farm;[27] however, after agreeing to participate in the fix, he became greedy. The original agreement between these four men and a gambler named Joseph Sullivan stated that the players would receive $80,000 ($10,000 each) if they could guarantee that eight players would participate in throwing the series. After the players closed this deal with Sullivan, Cicotte and Gandil offered the same proposition to another gambler, Arnold Rothstein. Instead of receiving $80,000, however, the players demanded $100,000.[28] Rothstein agreed, and all that was left to do was to convince four more players to participate.

These four conspirators coaxed the other four participants—"Happy" Felsch, "Lefty" Williams, "Shoeless" Joe Jackson, and "Buck" Weaver—into losing the World Series by telling them the fix would happen with or without them. During the players' trial, Happy Felsch confessed:

> I didn't want to get in on the deal at first . . . . But when they let me in on the idea, too many men were involved. I didn't like to be a squealer and I knew that if I stayed out of the deal and said nothing they would go ahead without me and I'd be that much money out without accomplishing anything.[29]

Lefty Williams gave the same reason as Felsch for participating in the fix. Gandil presented the situation clearly to Williams: if he cooperated, he'd earn $10,000; if he didn't, he would receive nothing and the team would lose the series anyway. Although both Jackson and Weaver agreed to throw the series for the same reasons as Felsch and Williams, their performances in the World Series do not reflect their decisions to participate. Jackson, for example, had a .375 average for the World Series, the highest on his team.[30] Gandil offered Jackson $10,000 to participate, and then $20,000.[31] Jackson refused both times. After Gandil nagged him continuously, however, Jackson finally agreed to the proposition. It is evident, however, that Jackson was not an active participant. He neither attended meetings with gamblers nor purposely attempted to lose any of the games.[32] Nevertheless, Jackson received $5,000 from the gamblers.[33] Buck Weaver also had an excellent Series, batting .324[34] and committing no errors,[35] but he received no money from the gamblers.[36] Though he had at first agreed to the fix and had attended two meetings with the gamblers, Weaver changed his mind, openly expressed his disapproval of the fix and defied the gamblers by playing to his potential. Author Eliot Asinot wrote about Weaver: "There was no bitterness, no hatred no frustration powerful enough to corrupt his love for baseball!"[37] Though Buck Weaver played his best and received nothing in the fix, he eventually received the same severe punishment given to the other seven players by the commissioner.

After the Series the eight players continued playing for the White Sox. Late in the season of 1920, however, a grand jury handed down indictments against them and the public learned of the scandal. Baseball fans' dismay at the fixing of the 1919 World Series and their new reluctance to go see games greatly diminished baseball's popularity and threatened its future. Fans had always put great faith in baseball players. Now the World Series scandal destroyed this confidence.[38] In 1921, a writer in *The Nation* stated:

> We do not trust cashiers half so much, or diplomats, or policeman or physicians, as we trust an outfielder or a shortstop . . . the one thing he is not called is a sneak or a traitor. The man at bat is supposed to be doing his best . . . . To find out that famous players have been corrupted is more than to lose faith in them personally; it is to begin to doubt the whole system . . . .[39]

Fans did not blame only the eight players involved in the fix. They reasoned that if there was corruption on one team, there was probably corruption on other teams as well.[40] Fans, therefore, no longer wanted to pay to see games they suspected were fixed, and their grievances did not end with the players. Many fans complained about the National Commission, a group of three men who governed baseball prior to 1921.[41] Although both fans and baseball officials had felt that the National Commission was weak, they now blamed it for not being able to protect the players from gamblers.[42] They also claimed that if the National Commission had been an organized, powerful body, officials would have known of the scandal earlier and they would have been able to impose punishments faster.[43] Thus, because fans were angry at both the players and the governing body of the game, team owners decided they needed a new system of power in baseball.

Baseball's new system of government consisted of a commissioner. The appointment of baseball's first commissioner is attributed to a prominent businessman named Albert Lasker. Lasker believed club owners were not capable of ruling baseball.[44] Instead, he proposed that, because baseball belonged to the public, the owners should chose a man financially detached from baseball to govern it.[45] This commissioner should have the power to impose fines on both players and owners.[46] Although Lasker proposed his plan before the World Series scandal, he received little support for it until 1921, when owners finally realized the need for change.[47] In 1921, the owners chose Kenesaw Mountain Landis, a prominent judge, for their first commissioner. Coincidentally, in the same year the eight players were brought to trial for conspiracy. Even before the trial, Landis had sworn, "there (was) no chance for any (of the eight players) to creep back into baseball."[48] Landis fulfilled his promise. A few months later, though a jury acquitted the players, Landis issued this statement:

> Regardless of the verdict of juries, no player who throws a ball game, no player that undertakes or promises to throw a ballgame, no player that sits in conference with a bunch of crooked players and gamblers, where the ways and means of throwing a game are discussed and does not promptly tell his club about it, will ever play professional baseball again![49]

After imposing this punishment, Landis was regarded as a hero who cleaned up baseball.[50] Landis remained adamant in his decision for punishment. Five months after the trial, Buck Weaver asked Landis for reinstatement. Landis' reply (which he issued to the press, not Weaver) stated "birds of a feather flock together. Men associating with gamblers and crooks (can) expect no leniency."[51] Though a jury had acquitted the eight players of conspiracy, baseball's first commissioner, after promising to rid baseball of corruption,[52] prohibited the players from playing baseball ever again.

Thus, because fixed games existed long before 1919, because team owner Charles Comiskey paid his players unfairly, and because some of the players who disapproved of the scheme, nevertheless, did not want to be excluded from it, eight members of the Chicago White Sox agreed to lose the World Series of 1919. This scandal threatened the future of baseball until 1921, when baseball's first commissioner, Judge Landis, imposed severe punishments on the eight players in an effort to convince angry fans that he was purifying the game. In a way, the scandal of 1919 was inevitable because of the prevalence of corruption and the weakness of baseball's officials. Fortunately, Landis became involved in the situation. Some people argue that Landis' punishments, particularly of Weaver and Jackson, were too harsh. But Landis was correct. Had he allowed Jackson and Weaver to continue playing, he probably would not have convinced fans that baseball was once again clean. Landis needed to prove that he would not allow any player even remotely associated with corruption to stay in the game. Landis also sent the message to other players that he would tolerate no further corruption. Thus, President Taft was correct in stating baseball was a "clean, straight game." It never had been before, but because Landis intervened, he saved the game from self-destructing.

NOTES

[1] Harold Seymour, Baseball: The Golden Years (New York: Oxford University Press, 1971) 274.

[2] Eliot Asinof, Eight Men Out (New York: Holt, Rinehart and Winston, 1963) 10.

[3] Harold Seymour, Baseball: The Early Years (New York: Oxford University Press, 1960) 53.

[4] Asinof 13.

[5] Asinof 13.

[6] Seymour, The Early Years 53.

[7] Seymour, The Early Years 54.

[8] Hugh Fullerton, "Baseball on Trial," The New Republic 20 Oct. 1920: 184.

[9] Donald Gropman, Say It Ain't So, Joe! (Boston: Little, Brown and Co., 1979) 164.

[10] Glenn Dickey, The History of the World Series Since 1903 (New York: Stein and Day Publishers, 1984) 63.

[11] Fullerton 184.

[12] Gropman 183.

[13] Dickey 63.

[14] Dickey 63.

[15] Asinof 16.

[16] Asinof 22.

[17] Asinof 21.

[18] Asinof 51.

[19] Asinof 51.

[20] Asinof 21.

[21] Asinof 16.

[22] Asinof 16.

[23] Joe Reichler, The World Series: 76th Anniversary Edition (New York: Simon and Schuster, 1979) 147.

[24] Seymour, The Golden Years 332.

[25] Asinof 17.

[26] "White Sox Players Are All Acquitted by Chicago Jury," New York Times 3 Aug. 1921: 2.

[27] Asinof 16–17.

[28] Asinof 27.

[29] Asinof 190.

[30] John Durant, Highlights of the World Series (New York: Hastings House Publishers, 1973) 83.

[31] Gropman 163.

[32] Asinof 253.

[33] Dickey 68.

[34] Durant 83.

[35] Seymour, The Golden Years 333.

[36] Dickey 68.

[37] Asinof 63.

[38] Durant 55.

[39] "The Baseball Scandal," The Nation 13 Oct. 1920: 395, as quoted in Durant 55.

[40] "Scandal" 396.

[41] Asinof 200.

[42] Asinof 200.

[43] Asinof 200.

[44] Seymour, The Golden Years 311.

[45] Seymour, The Golden Years 312.

[46] Seymour, The Golden Years 312.

[47] Seymour, The Golden Years 312.

[48] Seymour, The Golden Years 323.

[49] Gropman 201.

[50] Seymour, The Golden Years 339.

[51] Seymour, The Golden Years 339.

[52] Asinof 280.

BIBLIOGRAPHY

Asinof, Eliot. Eight Men Out. New York: Holt, Rinehart and Winston, 1963.

"The Baseball Scandal." The Nation 13 Oct. 1920: 395–396.

Dickey, Glenn. The History of the World Series Since 1903. New York: Stein and Day Pub., 1984.

Durant, John. Highlights of the World Series. New York: Hastings House Pub., 1984.

Fullerton, Hugh. "Baseball on Trial." The New Republic 20 Oct. 1920: 183–184.

Gropman, Donald. Say It Ain't So Joe! Boston: Little, Brown and Co., 1979.

Reichler, Joe. The World Series 76th Anniversary Edition. New York: Simon and Schuster, 1979.

Seymour, Harold. Baseball: The Early Years. New York: Oxford University Press, 1960.

Seymour, Harold. Baseball: The Golden Years. New York: Oxford University Press, 1971.

"White Sox Players Are All Acquitted By a Chicago Jury." New York Times 3 Aug. 1921: 2.

APPENDIX B

In Order: The Value of Hierarchies for Primates

Gillian Steel
Expository Writing
June 13, 1990

CONTENTS

Thesis Statement: Primates who live in troops use both agonistic and dominant behavior to create within their group a social hierarchy that determines individual functions, which eliminate indecision and unnecessary fighting, thus increasing the group's chance for survival.

  I. Using aggressive behavior and specific signs of dominance, primates determine a hierarchy within the group where the most dominant animal has control over the lesser animals.
    A. Dominance is most clearly determined by physical characteristics, including strength, physical size, and size of canines, all three of which may demonstrate the ability to fight.
    B. Primates use aggressive movements and signals in an attempt to impose their superiority on other members of the group.
    C. Although primates use violent contact to demonstrate their dominance, many of the signals that primates use are not violent, but continue to demonstrate dominance.
    D. Lip smacking, grooming, and "grins," used to show friendliness, also demonstrate the more subordinate animals' submission.
 II. The structure of the hierarchy ensures that the most dominant animals have the most rights, along with the most responsibilities, while the lesser animals have the least amount of rights and the most obligations to their superiors.
    A. The most dominant animals have the most responsibilities to the group as a whole, but they also have the benefit of first choice in everything from food to sleeping quarters and choice of mates.
    B. In contrast, the lower members of the troop not only have the last pick in everything but also are obligated to repay their superiors by giving them food and by grooming them for longer periods of time.
    C. Although the troop is one united hierarchy, there are separate pecking orders within each of the sexes that reinforce the general structure.
III. Predetermined functions within the group make it much easier to make decisions in times of emergencies and to save the troop from a state of constant disagreement.
    A. In the confusion that naturally exists in times of danger, the troop needs a governing body that will direct it out of danger to avoid chaos and ultimately death of members of the troop.
    B. Preexisting functions also help to determine physical placement of individual members during times of defense to insure the protection of females and the young.
    C. Without the hierarchy within the troop there would be constant bickering among members, with much wasted energy and unnecessary fighting.

The underlying "cement" that keeps a group of primates together as one troop is the desire and need to be protected.[1] Primates organize a specific ranking order of all the members of their particular troop so that one animal, or a small clique, holds the most dominant position;[2] this one animal, or the small clique, is responsible for the group's safety. There is a continual process of defining individual rank within the hierarchy by displays of dominance. Often the display redefines the ranks when one animal attempts to attain a higher position in order to be "the dominant male" ultimately. This struggle ensures that the dominant male will be the best fighter because it weeds out the weaker members. A dominant figure eliminates vacillation in decision making and provides a patrol among group members, thus making it easier to protect the group from outsiders. Different species may vary in their particular behaviors, but the general pattern is the same amongst all primates.

To create and maintain a hierarchical system, primates engage in a certain amount of agonistic behavior, that is, behavior in which they struggle with each other for the sole purpose of gaining power. The more aggressive the species of primate is naturally, the more fighting goes on among the members of the troop in their ascent to the role of dominant male.[3] Although this behavior seems destructive to the group's relations at first, "mild antagonism does not disturb the bonds (between animals) but actually makes them stronger."[4] Aggression by itself would be detrimental to the group's relations, but because the group members rely on their superiors for protection, aggression from them reinforces the hierarchical bonds.[5]

Most clearly, dominance is determined by physical characteristics, including strength, physical size, and size of canine teeth, all three of which may demonstrate the ability to fight. Primates show strength not only when two animals confront each other, but also when one animal acts alone, as in the famous chimpanzee "charging displays" where males swing huge branches, even small trees, in violent display of their dominance.[6] The mere look of a particular animal, especially if he is a full-grown male, may scare some of the other troop members because large size often implies strength. The main fighting tool of the primate is the canine tooth. Located near the front teeth, the canine, often called the cuspid, is the longest tooth in a primate's mouth. It is often used during fights as the scars of many subordinate baboons testify.[7] (See Appendix, Figures 2 and 3.) Logically, the animal with the best combination of these three characteristics is almost always the most dominant member of the troop.

Primates also use aggressive movements and signals in an attempt to impose their superiority on other members of the troop. This agonistic behavior can be used either in defense of an established rank or in the ascent to a higher position. Because the size and strength of the dominant male may scare off many animals attempting to rival his position, there is much more fighting among the lower ranking animals whose positions are not so well defined.[8] These animals often fight, both playfully as juveniles and seriously as young adults. Anything from swipes of an arm to long, angry battles with scratching and biting can constitute a fight. A fight begins with the animals' slapping the ground and charging each other; then one will finally pin the other and bite him.[9] The most common type of "violence" within the troop is the punishment of the young juveniles. In reprimanding a young adult, the dominant animal usually gives a weak bite on the thick skin of the neck, hard enough to make sure the juvenile remembers but not so much so as to hurt him permanently. (See Appendix, Figure 1.)

Although primates use violent contact to demonstrate their dominance, they also use nonviolent signals. These signs include many threats of violence; in fact, "most aggression comprises mere threats."[10] Facial expressions reflect increasing amounts of aggression when two animals confront one another. For example, an angry baboon trying to express his own dominance will first stare down his opponent. Opening his eyes wider and wider, he begins to pull back the skin of his scalp and his ears. If his rival continues to be a nuisance, the baboon stands erect, with the hair of his mane on end.[11] (See Appendix, Figure 5.) Most likely, this behavior will be enough to persuade the other animal to stop what he is doing or to go away, so no violence occurs. Sometimes there is no direct confrontation between two members of the troop, but one male may mount the other, as he would a female; "(m)ounting is the supreme assertion of dominance."[12]

If violence does occur, "major fights are followed by a wave of grooming and other friendly contacts among the members of a group."[13] Lip smacking, grooming, and "grins," used to show friendliness, also demonstrate the more subordinate animals' submission. Primates often smack their lips when approaching another member of the troop to show they mean no harm. Even dominant males smack their lips as they advance toward a female with a new-born infant. When being attacked, an animal may smack his lips to show he gives in.[14] Lip smacking acknowledges the hierarchy that has already been established; however, it does not change any animal's position. A primate grins (a "fear grin") only to a more dominant animal to display submission; the more dominant animal never grins at his inferior.[15] As mounting is the supreme act of dominance, lowering the hind quarters is the supreme act of submission. Admitting submission avoids the pain of punishment; thus an inferior animal is likely to give in to the aggressive members of the troop.

As a result of these signals and contacts between members of the troop, there exists a hierarchy, a clique of dominant males at the top and juveniles at the bottom. The most dominant animals have the most responsibilities to the group as a whole, but they also have the benefit of first choice in everything from food to sleeping quarters and choice of mates. The dominant males act both as the mediators of general interactions and as a governing body to make decisions for the troop. They lead the troop in all of the daily activities and keep watch for predators; they are the last animals to go to sleep each night. During the day, they try to keep the groups' fighting to a minimum, as most primates have a tendency to bicker. They are rewarded for their services by getting more of everything they want. Dominant males have the most and best sleeping space, whether it be a larger tree or a wider rock. When the troop eats, they eat first, ensuring that they get the most food. Dominant males can also choose any mate from among the females. In fact, only the dominant male can mate in public view.[16] The ultimate benefit is a longer life span; the best of everything in combination with an already physically fit animal produces a healthy and long life.[17]

In contrast, the lowest members of the hierarchy not only have the last pick in everything but also are obligated to repay their superiors by giving them any food they want and by grooming them for longer periods of time than they are groomed themselves. For example, scientists threw tangerines between two macaques: A, the more dominant, and B, his subordinate. No matter where the tangerine fell, A always ate it. Even when the tangerine fell right at B's feet, A took it and ate it. Not until after A was full, and only after he had mounted B, did A allow B to eat a tangerine. The lowest members of the troop must also groom their superiors for the longest periods of time. It is not uncommon to see the mate of a dominant male groom him for twenty minutes, only to be rewarded with thirty seconds of grooming herself. (See Appendix, Figure 4.) Afterwards, the male often turns around again to be groomed for a little while longer.[18]

Although the troop is one united hierarchy, there are separate pecking orders within each troop that reinforce the general structure. Any female is necessarily subordinate to all the adult males of the troop. Different criteria for each sex determine the rank of an individual. "It is a well established fact that hierarchies among female macaques are virtually independent of weight, physical condition, and other indicators of fighting ability,"[19] whereas in males, fighting ability is the main determining factor. From the time they are weaned, males are on their own to fight out a position in their hierarchy. They play-fight with each other first; then as they get bigger, they fight with some of the older animals, slowly working their way toward the dominant position. They also playfight with the females, but with time the young males learn to control aggression toward the females,[20] especially those females that are protected by a dominant male. The female, however, has a higher or lower rank depending originally on her family's status, then on the rank of her mate as well.

The hierarchical structure and predetermined status make it easy for the dominant males to control the group, so there are minimal confusion and chaos during everyday life and in threatening situations. In the confusion that naturally occurs in times of danger, the troop needs a governing body that will direct it out of danger to avoid chaos and ultimately the deaths of members of the troop. If a predator threatens, the troop needs someone to tell it where to go; if it were left up to the troop as a whole, individuals would scatter in different directions and some would be abandoned and killed. The dominant male's position allows one individual to determine the best course of action and to follow through with it. There was once a case in which hunters killed the dominant gorilla. The other members of the group, too afraid to move, sat in one place. Consequently, the hunters slaughtered the entire troop.[21] The structure of the hierarchy forces the dominant male to direct the group while assigning the task of protecting individuals to another, less dominant member of the troop. This behavior guarantees that the greatest number of animals will survive.

Preexisting functions also help to determine physical placement of individual members during times of defense to assure the protection of the females and the young. During daily life the troop eats, sleeps, and travels in the same pattern as exists when the troop is under attack. The dominant males stay close to the females and the young, while the less dominant males form a shield for them, and finally, out in front the young troop members keep a lookout, partially because they are the most expendable members of the troop.[22] If there seems to be danger ahead, the dominant males signal to the others to stay clear; then they drop back to form a protective shield.[23] If there were no ranking system, not only would many of the young males try to fight the predator and be killed themselves or cause the death of another troop member, but there would also be no one to protect the females and the young.

Without a hierarchical system, the troop would have constant bickering among members with much wasted energy and unnecessary fighting. Primates tend to bicker among themselves constantly. Small fights break out periodically, but the majority of disagreements are settled quickly by the obvious dominance of one animal over another. For example, if a juvenile baboon tries to bother a female, a more dominant male will often take charge and scare the juvenile away. If there weren't a hierarchical system and the juvenile bothered the female, then when the other male arrived, the two would have to fight to see who would get his way. No one would be in charge in times of emergency, so all the animals in the troop would scatter, making them obvious prey. The males who try to defend the group, or themselves, would have no energy with which to do so because they would have spent it all fighting the males in their own troop.[24] The hierarchical system is therefore advantageous because it allows the most able animals to defend the group.

The hierarchical system supports Darwin's theory of the survival of the fittest. Primates who live in troops increase the group's chance for survival by using agonistic and dominant behavior to create a social

hierarchy that determines individual functions, thus eliminating indecision and unnecessary fighting. The hierarchical scenario is uncan-
nily like the business world that many of us know today. The president
is dominant over the vice-presidents, the vice-president is dominant
over the supervisors, and so on down the line to the mail room clerk.
The power that goes with being president of a company allows that
person to fly first class, eat caviar, and choose a spouse among many
eager men and women. On the other hand, this person must run the
business smoothly and also protect it from mergers and takeovers.
Patterns in the business world resemble those of baboons in times of
trouble. The similarities between the two societies can be seen not
only in the human business arena but also in our social circles. Early in
human development, perhaps even as early as kindergarten, cliques
emerge among children; a central figure becomes dominant, and he
or she begins to set trends and to boss around the other children.
Situations like this can arise among people of all ages, anywhere in
the world from the United States to China to Brazil. By studying animal
behavior, we may be able to learn more about our own social patterns, why people everywhere act in a certain way. "The study of animal behavior sheds light on the roots of our own societies."[25]

NOTES

[1] Irven DeVore and Sarel Eimerl, The Primates (New York: Time-Life Books, 1970) 110.

[2] Stephen Phillip Easley, Anthony M. Coelho, Jr., and Linda L. Taylor, "Allogrooming, Partner Choice and Dominance in Male Annubis Baboons," American Journal of Physical Anthropology 80 (1989): 353.

[3] DeVore and Eimerl 131.

[4] Frans De Waal, Peacemaking Among Primates (Cambridge, MA: Harvard University Press, 1989) 15.

[5] De Waal 15.

[6] Jane Van Lawick-Goodall, In the Shadow of Man (Boston: Houghton Mifflin Company, 1971) 28.

[7] DeVore and Eimerl 116.

[8] DeVore and Eimerl 119.

[9] Irven DeVore, Primate Behavior (Chicago: Holt, Rinehart and Winston, 1965) 100.

[10] De Waal 101.

[11] DeVore and Eimerl 108.

[12] DeVore and Eimerl 106.

[13] De Waal 15.

[14] DeVore 106.

[15] Van Lawick-Goodal 68.

[16] De Waal 131.

[17] De Waal 128.

[18] DeVore and Eimerl 107.

[19] De Waal 94.

[20] De Waal 11.

[21] DeVore and Eimerl 111.

[22] DeVore and Eimerl 139.

[23] De Vore and Eimerl 139.

[24] DeVore 59.

[25] De Waal 127.

APPENDIX

[In the original paper, the appendix contained photographs, which were credited as follows.]

Fig. 1. Frans De Waal, Peacemaking Among Primates (Cambridge, MA: Harvard University Press, 1989) 15.

Fig. 2. Irven DeVore and Sarel Eimerl, The Primates (New York: Time-Life Books, 1970) 116.

Fig. 3. DeVore and Eimerl 116.

Fig. 4. De Waal 28.

Fig. 5. De Waal 31.

BIBLIOGRAPHY

Ardrey, Robert. The Territorial Imperative. New York: McClelland and Stewart Ltd., 1968.

Denny, M. Ray. Comparative Psychology: An Evolutionary Analysis of Animal Behavior. New York: John Wiley and Sons, 1980.

DeVore, Irven. Primate Behavior. Chicago: Holt, Rinehart and Winston, 1965.

DeVore Irven and Sarel Eimerl. The Primates. New York: Time-Life Books, 1970.

De Waal, Frans. Peacemaking Among Primates. Cambridge, MA: Harvard University Press, 1989.

Hahn, Emily. On the Side of the Apes. New York: Thomas Y. Crowell Company, 1971.

Kohler, Wolfgang. The Mentality of Apes. London: Redwood Press, 1973.

Lorenz, Konrad. On Aggression. New York: Harcourt Brace Jovanovich, 1966.

Marler, Peter R., ed. The Marvels of Animal Behavior. Washington, DC: The National Geographic Society, 1976.

Prince, J. H. The Universal Urge. Nashville: Thomas Nelson, Inc., 1972.

Van Lawick-Goodall, Jane. In the Shadow of Man. Boston: Houghton Mifflin Company, 1971.

APPENDIX C

---◇---

A.D. 547–1536: The Golden Age of Monasticism?

Louisa Anne Burnham
Expository Writing
December 12, 1980

CONTENTS

Thesis Statement: Although the institution of monasticism contributed greatly to medieval life through a distribution of charity and the atmosphere of learning and culture that surrounded it, the daily life of the individual monastery was often rendered corrupt by the frequent bypassing, both by the abbots and the monastic community in general, of the traditions and the way of life established by St. Benedict's Rule.

I. Medieval society benefited from the presence of the monasteries because of the charity and hospitality they distributed to the poor and travelers, and because of the many intellectual and cultural contributions they had to offer.
   A. According to monastic tradition, the monks offered charity by means of guest houses and meals to the poor and to travelers, thus benefiting much of the population.
   B. The monasteries were also great centers for intellectual and cultural growth; the monks were among the most educated people in the world, and they initiated a great many of the important advances in literature, architecture, and music.

II. The abbot, the most important member of any monastic community, was gradually forced to relinquish his role as the father of the community; in order to fulfill his obligations as a feudal lord, he could no longer live as an ordinary monk nor set a good example to his fellow monks.
   A. As his monastery began to possess more and more land, and as his feudal and administrative responsibilities increased, the medieval abbot found himself to be increasingly estranged from the ordinary life of his abbey.
   B. Since the abbot was the very "pivot on which the life of the monastery turned," if he were a strong, spiritual man, the monastery would follow suit, but conversely, if he were weak, or highly secular, the monks could do (and did) as they pleased.

III. The high ideals set forth in the monastic Rules were often rendered corrupt by not being followed word for word and were sometimes abandoned almost entirely.
   A. Since they followed the secular example set by the abbots, it was a common sight to see monks wandering through the medieval countryside, a direct affront to St. Benedict's Rule, which dictates strict confinement to the monastery.
   B. Ignoring the precept of poverty, which implies a complete renunciation of personal property, most medieval monks had possessions, ranging from costume jewelry to slaves, and varying amounts of money.
   C. By tradition, and St. Benedict's Rule, butcher's meat was forbidden to the monks except under certain conditions such as sick-

ness or meals with guests, and eating was, at all times, to be in moderation; in actuality, however, monks were commonly satirized as gluttons, and meat was a standard part of their diet.

D. In disregard of the old Benedictine principle *ora et labora*, pray and work, virtually all monks had ceased any heavy manual labour by the medieval period and were primarily idle.

E. The sexual immorality of the monks, while not universal, nor as widespread as some of the other corruptions mentioned above, still existed to a significant degree; the fact that it existed at all is disturbing.

The Age of Faith, The Golden Age of Monasticism—epithets that are commonly applied to the European Middle Ages. They evoke in our minds a time of great Christian feeling, a time when the lives of most people revolved around the Church, and when a person of deep religious convictions naturally gravitated toward life in a monastic community, living piously in prayer and holy labor. Not so, for most inhabitants of medieval monasteries were not the devout and devoted individuals we often consider them to be; many were younger sons of nobles, with family property entailed away from them by primogeniture, who had no choice but to enter a monastery. Others were noble bastards, whose fathers wished them out of the way at a minimum expense, or criminals, for whom the tonsure was an alternative to prison.[1] Consequently, the pious and holy ideals of monastic life were very often set aside, the monks seeming to be rather members of a "rich bachelor fraternity"[2] than the spiritual and self-denying men they were supposed to be. In spite of the general irreligious atmosphere and the many infractions of the monastic Rules the overall influence of the many abbeys and priories was positive, for they provided the opportunity to learn and study in a society where intellectual knowledge was usually secondary (especially among the lower classes) to physical prowess. The monks were also the medieval equivalent of a welfare and hostel system: they distributed alms and food to the needy and poor, and the monastery guest house was the temporary home of many travelers. The façade of the monasteries of Medieval Europe is that of a solid institution that benefited society. A closer look, however, reveals the many corruptions with which it was riddled. The gradual decline from the grand monastic tradition of St. Benedict's Rule, the first, and greatest, of the monastic Rules, and the secularization which accompanied it were typical of medieval monachism.

Despite this gradual deterioration of the monastic ideals during the Middle Ages, the Church in general, and the monasteries in particular, were the primary source of aid to the needy. According to monastic tradition, the monks offered charity in the form of food and alms to the poor, and hospitality by means of guest houses and meals to travelers, thus benefiting much of the population. In the medieval era society consisted primarily of two classes: the very rich and the very poor. During times of famine and distress the poor were often left completely desolate, and the monasteries were a place of refuge for them, providing a home and food. *The Chronicle of Evesham*, written in England shortly after the Conqueror, states that during one disaster "a vast multitude of men old and young, and of women with their little ones, came to Evesham in their distress, fleeing from famine, all these Aethilwild (the Abbot) supported as best he could."[3] But the monasteries were sources of relief not only during isolated times of distress, for almost every day of the year was a day of need to the very poor, and the monks serviced this need also. They distributed alms through a daily dole, and any extras from the monastic table were given to the poor. One famous Rule, the *Regularis Concordia* (the Regular Canons were one of the larger Orders in England during this period), stipulates that "accommodation and livelihood should be provided by each monastery for a certain number of the poor."[4] The other important charitable contribution the monks had to offer was that of their guest houses. All pilgrims, whether traveling relatively short distances or making long journeys, stayed at the monastic "hotels," and many other travelers did also, because the only cost of accommodation was any contribution the guest might make to the monastic funds. In all, between 3–10% of the total monachal income was given out as charity in one form or another,[5] a substantial contribution when it is considered how rich many of these monasteries were.

Charity was not the only contribution medieval monachism had to make; the monasteries were also great centers for intellectual and cultural growth, for the monks were among the most educated people in the world, and they initiated a great many of the important advances in literature, architecture and music. Close examination of a list of important medieval books reveals the many famous monastic authors. Books such as *The Anglo-Saxon Chronicle* (a history of the Church ranging from its early years to 1154), the writings of the Venerable Bede (an early English monk who wrote on a variety of subjects), *The Chronicle of Jocelin de Brakelond* (a chronicle of St. Edmund's Abbey at Bury, and particularly of its Abbot, Samson, as recorded by his chaplain Jocelin), and the famous book *Of the Imitation of Christ* by Thomas à Kempis, a German monk, are quite probably the most important books of the Middle Ages, for they show us the human side of medieval life and religion. But it is not only as actual authors that the monks exhibit their influence on literature. The hundreds of exquisite manuscripts of the Bible and other spiritual works, such as the prayerbook illustrated in Plate I*, all proclaim the skill of the monks working in the scriptorii. Also, the monastic libraries were the principal depositories of books during the medieval period,[6] often having as many as 300–600 books.[7] Another important artistic contribution of the monks was their interest in architecture. They built magnificent churches and chapterhouses, the most famous of which is probably Westminster Abbey (Plate II) or Canterbury Cathedral (Plate III) in England, with Mont St. Michel in Brittany not far behind (Plate IV). Their buildings were masterpieces of Gothic architecture, with tall spires reaching to the sky, glorious arched ceilings, and stained glass windows. It was in the choirs of these spacious churches where another of the monachal contributions was appreciated: music. The medieval Church music was the very beginning of modern music. The Gregorian Chant, a single line of melody sung to the words of a prayer (the Kyrie, or the Magnificat, for example), was

---

*The author interleaved illustrations in the original essay.

the first serious attempt at music since Roman times, but gradually composers began to write in harmony, generally for three voices. This Church music, well preserved because of the superior monastic scribes who were able to record the music for posterity, was the beginning of modern polyphony and is one of the most important monastic contributions of the Middle Ages,[8] along with the more tangible Church buildings and manuscripts. As can be seen, the monks in medieval times left us many bequests, not least among them these advances in literature, architecture, and music.

Despite the beneficial influence the monasteries had upon medieval society, they were not perfect. The feudal system was sweeping Europe at this time, and the monasteries were not left unaffected. As his monastery began to possess more and more land, the medieval abbot found himself to be increasingly estranged from the ordinary life of his abbey. As a feudal lord, and vassal, the abbot was expected to be present at his lord's court, often that of the King, which took him away from his cloister for long stretches of time.[9] The Rule of St. Benedict, the most influential of the medieval Rules, stipulates that although the abbot has almost unlimited power, and is the most important person in the abbey,[10] he is to live as an ordinary member of the community;[11] the only exceptions to this rule were that the abbot was allowed to sleep not in the common dormitory, but in his own private room, and that he was allowed to dine not at the communal table of the refectory but instead with any guests the monastery might have. But, as time went by, many abbots bypassed these simple, practical exemptions from the Rule, and with the excuse of feudal duties, took advantage of them. The abbot's "room apart" gradually became a complete establishment consisting of his own hall, court, garden (Plate V—prior's establishment) and a chapel where he heard mass daily instead of reciting the office with the community.[12] His "baronial dignity"[13] often expressed itself in what one historian terms "palatial lodgings"[14] that often included great parks and country houses. Even Abbot Samson, the hero of Jocelin's Chronicle, spent a great deal of time away from the abbey at his manor at Melford, proclaiming that he preferred country life.[15] This secularization, which caused the abbots of a landed monastery to seem to be barons rather than anything resembling monks, was reflected in the qualities looked for in the choice of an abbot. By the "middle" of the Middle Ages, the first choice was no longer someone extraordinarily saintly and pious, but rather someone who possessed great business acumen. In the words of Sir Arthur Bryant:

> The age of monastic saints had passed; what was now admired in conventual circles was a dignified, shrewd man of the world who combined the conventional Christian virtues with a keen eye for his house's interests.[16]

In fact, many abbots were appointed by a lord or king, as opposed to having been elected by their monks, and were entirely unsuited for spiritual office. Abbot Roger is an example: after his appointment by the king to the position of abbot at Evesham Abbey in 1189, the power of his office went to his head, and he was eventually deposed as a petty tyrant, having starved the monks and committed other sins.[17] Even those chosen by their own communities were by the 12th century less pious than abbots had been in the early days of monasticism; Samson was generally acknowledged to be "more of an administrator than an ecclesiastic"[18] and at the siege of Windsor was, in the words of Jocelin, who admired him very greatly, "more remarkable there for his counsel than for his piety."[19] Samson was typical of his age: a skillful administrator as opposed to a pious saint, who enjoyed the privileges his office gave him, and took full advantage of them.

The importance of the secularization of the abbots, and the far-reaching consequences it had, can be understood when one realizes the influence the character of an abbot had upon his monastery. Since the abbot was the very "pivot on which the life of the mastery turned,"[20] his character had a great effect on the monks; if he were a strong, spiritual man, the monastery would follow suit, but conversely, if he were either weak, or highly secular, the monks could do (and did) as they pleased. According to St. Benedict's Rule, the abbot should be the very center of the monastic life and no major decisions could be made without his approval. He should also set an example for his monks "in deeds rather than words all that is good and holy."[21] When the abbot did set an example of goodness and holiness, as Abbot Samson of Bury St. Edmunds did, the monastery prospered. Despite the financial mess it had fallen into under the previous Abbot, Hugh, Samson pulled the monastery out of deep debt through his example of paying back debts, not borrowing any more money, and not spending more than necessary. Hugh had been old, and had grown weak, and thus had not kept track of his monks' business matters. A quotation from Jocelin's *Chronicle* says it very aptly:

> Abbot Hugh had by this time grown old . . . ; pious and kindly he was, but neither good nor provident in this world's business . . . . in the external matters, things were going badly, for, since they were serving under a lord that was simple and growing old, every man did as he wished, not as he ought.[22]

For the monks of St. Edmunds, doing as they wished seemed to indicate overspending the money allotted to them for their crafts, and subsequently going into debt. The sacristan alone had sealed £3,052 in debts under Abbot Hugh,[23] but when Samson became abbot, the debts were uncovered and paid back, and the culprit was deposed. Abbot Hugh himself had placed the Abbey into debt for over £2,300,[24] mostly to Jews, who charged interest, as opposed to Christians, who did not, setting a poor example for his monks, who, as it has been demonstrated, followed it. The principle that the abbot should hold "Christ's place"[25] in the monastery was *sometimes* followed; what was *always* true, however, was that when an abbot set an example, the monks followed it.

The monks *did* follow the abbatial example, with the result that the high ideals set forth in the monastic Rules were often rendered corrupt by not being followed word for word, and were sometimes abandoned almost entirely. Just how corrupt the monasteries were can be seen by examining several common infractions of the Rule, and seeing how extensive they were. One of the most common, and certainly among the most commented on by contemporaries was the frequent absence of the monks from their monasteries, sometimes on feudal business, but more often on trips for pleasure. Since they followed the secular example set by the abbots, it was a common sight to see monks wandering through the medieval countryside, a direct affront to St. Benedict's Rule, which dictates strict confinement to the monastery. All monastic sources point to cloisterization as something necessary for the good of the monastery: St. Benedict decrees it in his Rule,[26] and St. Jerome, in describing the "model monk" states that this monk is only capable of living in his cloister, and once outside it, dies "like a fish out of water."[27] Examples of St. Jerome's model of monachal goodness were few and far between, and Chaucer, in the General Prologue of *The Canterbury Tales*, has the monk, out of his cloister for a pleasant spring pilgrimage to Canterbury, refute this monastic ideal:

> He did not rate that text at a plucked hen
> Which says that hunters are not holy men
> And that a monk uncloistered is a mere
> Fish out of water, flapping on the pier,
> That is to say, a monk out of his cloister.
> That was a text he held not worth an oyster.[28]

Although Chaucer was writing fiction, his writing is a comment on his society, and reflects the realities of the time, as does the very famous *Vision of Piers Plowman*, believed to have been written by William Langland in the 14th century, where the author laments:

> As now is Religioun a ryder, a rowmer bi stretes,
> A leder of love-dayes and a londe-buyer,
> A priker on a palfray fro manere to manere,
> An heep of houndes at his ers, as he a lorde were.[29]

These comments of the people (for Chaucer was not a cleric, and Langland is believed to have taken only minor orders) upon the state of monachism are very valuable, for they show that it is not only ourselves looking back who consider this aspect of monastic life corrupt. It is, however, also valuable to look back at statements of the monks themselves. In 1444, the English General Chapter of Benedictines imposed standard punishments for various offenses such as lying, or striking a fellow monk. Among them was the punishment of temporary conformity to the regulation of monastic confinement for periods ranging from three weeks to one year.[30] This decree is amusing when one considers that confinement to the cloister was supposed to be a permanent and integral part of the daily adherence to the Rule; obviously little attention was now paid to it. This example shows how widespread absence from the monasteries was, if even those in charge of monastic morals considered it usual, and did not try to curtail it, while inflicting punishments for other infractions.

Another corruption of monastic life was the absence of poverty among the monks. The "Three Substantials" of monachism were Poverty, Chastity, and Obedience, from which, supposedly, no monk could ever be released.[31] But ignoring this precept of poverty, which implies a complete renunciation of personal property, most medieval monks had possessions, ranging from costume jewelry to slaves, and varying amounts of money. Many flaunted their possessions openly: Chaucer's prioress—

> She wore a coral trinket on her arm,
> A set of beads, the gaudies tricked in green,
> Whence hung a golden brooch of brightest sheen
> On which there first was graven a crowned A,
> And lower, *Amor vincit omnia.*[32]

Even if one overlooks the *Amor vincit omnia* (love conquers all), her decoration is hardly monastic, and neither is that of her companion The Monk, of whom Chaucer says:

> He had a wrought gold cunningly fashioned pin;
> Into a lover's knot it seemed to pass.[33]

Such repeated observations of very unmonastic jewelry on monastics seem to underscore how commonplace such behavior was. Once again, a statement from a General Chapter inadvertently gives an insight on the frequency of unorthodox behavior—in this case, monks possessing slaves. The General Chapter of the Cistercians, a "reformed" monastic order, states:

> We decree, under pain of deposition and expulsion, that no person of this Order presume to purchase Saracen women as concubines to their Saracen slaves, for any cause whatsoever.[34]

Information that monks had personal slaves, and money to buy concubines for them is issued with no mention of shame. It thus appears that slaveholding was relatively commonplace and acceptable; only the purchase of concubines warranted punishment. The pocket-money the monks appear to have possessed came from various sources: some monks embezzled, like the sacristan at Bury St. Edmunds in 1185, who at his death was found to be in possession of a fortune.[35] Others accepted bribes, like Abbot Samson, for whom "ten marks, as it is said, 'did blind the eyes of the wise.'"[36] Possessions were widespread among monks; in some monasteries each monk had his own apartments[37] instead of the monks sharing a common dorter, and at Launceston, an English monastery of the Regular Canons, every canon had his own room, personal servant, dog, herb garden, and dovecote, as well as a cash allowance for trifles.[38] "Proprietary" monks, as they were termed in the Middle Ages,[39] were a very serious lesion in the body of the church, and contributed greatly to her corruption.

> Which, I ask, is the graver transgression in the matter of flesh-eating?
> That of the Black monks (Benedictines), who eat it openly, or of the
> White monks (Cistercians), who (as it is said) often eat it secretly to
> repletion? For both have the same Benedictine Rule.[40]

This quotation from the 14th century canonist John of Oyton states plainly how widespread the problem of monastic gluttony and flesh-eating was. By tradition, and St. Benedict's Rule, butcher's meat was forbidden to the monks except under certain conditions such as sickness or meals with guests,[41] and eating was, at all times, to be in moderation;[42] in actuality, however, monks were commonly satirized as gluttons, and meat was a standard part of their diet. By the High Middle Ages, the number of monks pretending to be sick, or merely eating at the infirmary, where they could get meat, had grown so great that by a papal decree, at any given time, one-half of the monks were allowed to eat meat in a place called the "misericord" just outside the infirmary.[43] Although in theory the monastic diet consisted of merely two cooked dishes, bread, fruit, and beer or wine[44] (not *haute cuisine* by any standards), the table of a well-off monastery was a byword for good dining.[45] As an example, the chronicler Abailard said:

> Every lean fellow, when he reacheth this stew pond of the cloister,
> soon waxeth so fat and well-liking that, seeing him again after a
> brief while, thou shalt scarce know him for what he was.[46]

The 12th century archdeacon and monastic critic Giraldus Cambrensis, Gerald of Wales, spoke a great deal about the gluttony of monks everywhere. In this passage he deplores the eating habits of the monks at Canterbury Cathedral because of the tendency of gluttony to corrupt the whole moral structure of the monastic system. It seems to sum up the problem of monastic gluttony quite well:

> This added heaven of gluttony proceeded forthwith to dissolve and
> corrupt the whole lump of pristine probity.[47]

As the feudal system took hold in medieval Europe, the monasteries grew increasingly rich, and as is the custom of people everywhere when they become wealthy, the monks gradually discontinued their manual toil. In disregard of the old Benedictine principle *ora et labora,* pray and work,[48] virtually all monks had ceased any heavy manual labor by the medieval period, and were primarily idle. All hard work was done by servants, the number of which often equaled, and sometimes exceeded, the number of monks.[49] These servants did all manual work except writing, manuscript copying, and any craft work the monks might do.[50] The work in the fields (which St. Benedict specifically mentions as a blessing for all monks[51]), cleaning, cooking—all were done by hired servants, lay brothers, or serfs.[52] This was deplored by several contemporary chroniclers who felt that this basic laziness was harmful to the spiritual atmosphere of the monastery and contrary to St. Benedict's statement that "idleness is an enemy of the soul."[53] One of these monastic chroniclers, Abailard, said:

> We, who ought to live by the labour of our own hands (which alone as St. Benedict saith maketh us truly monks), do now follow after idleness, that enemy of the soul, and seek our livelihood from the labours of other men.[54]

This relatively general statement condemning the common idleness of the monks is expanded upon by Peter the Venerable of Cluny who, in lamenting the corrupt nature of his own very famous "reformed" monastery, said:

> Idleness, which our Father St. Benedict calleth the enemy of the soul, had gotten such a hold upon a great number of our inmates, and especially upon the so-called lay brethren (brothers not having taken full orders; generally the ones who did the most manual work in a monastery) that, both within and without the cloister they either slept against the walls of the cloister or wasted the whole day, almost from sunrise to sunset—nay, almost into midnight, when they might do it with impunity—in vain, idle, and worse still, oftentimes in back biting talk.[55]

The continual sloth of these monks numbed both their bodies and their souls, defeating the purpose of the tenet of *ora et labora,* which was to stimulate the mind as well as the body by moderate labor,[56] and also to prevent instances such as the "backbiting talk" mentioned above.

The inactivity of the monks was reflected not only in immoral talk, but also in immoral actions.

> In many monasteries they led a carnal life; for the brethren, having no spiritual delights, sought those of the flesh.[57]

This quotation from Humbert de Romans, a 12th-century chronicler, is a sad commentary on the moral state of medieval monastic life. The sexual immorality of the monks, while not universal, nor as widespread as some of the other corruptions mentioned above, still existed to a significant degree; the fact that unchastity existed at all is disturbing. At the time of the Dissolution of the Monasteries in England (1536) some 251 persons were charged with "incontinence" and 189 with sodomy.[58] These figures were somewhat exaggerated by the "visitors" to the monasteries, who were, after all, trying to find reasons to disband them, but nonetheless, the figures are quite large, even when exaggeration is taken into account. Other contemporaries commented on the comparatively frequent unchastity of monks also; St. Odo of Cluny in 942 sadly declaimed that "the vow of chastity is only too commonly broken,"[59] and Giraldus Cambrensis relates the story of a knight making a pilgrimage to the shrine of St. James of Compostela in Spain who is told that "the monks of these parts keep their mistresses and lemans publicly; . . . the Order is not so strict hereabouts."[60] The names of those rumored to have sinned is endless: well-known personages such as the Abbot of Bardney,[61] the Abbot of Peterborough[62] and Abbot Roger of Evesham[63] are notorious examples. The violation of this one of the Three Substantials (Poverty, Chastity, and Obedience) is more serious than the violations of the others, for Poverty and Obedience were rules for monks only, while Chastity is one of the ten commandments and is therefore supposed to be a rule for everyone. The fact that the monks did not observe even the rule of chastity indicates how much they were drawn to the secular example, which further shows how immoral the monasteries had become.

Were the Middle Ages really the "Golden Age of Monasticism"? They started well enough in 547 with the writing of St. Benedict's Rule, which has dictated the precepts and ideals of monastic life ever since, but they ended ingloriously when Henry VIII dissolved the monasteries in 1536. What about the intervening years? Was the promise of the Rule carried out, or was there a steady downward path to the Dissolution? In fact, there was neither, but instead something of a compromise. Although the institution of monasticism contributed greatly to medieval life through a distribution of charity and the atmosphere of learning and culture which surrounded it, the daily life of the individual monastery was often rendered corrupt by the frequent bypassing, both by the abbots and the monastic community in general, of the traditions and the way of life established by St. Benedict's Rule.

NOTES

[1] George Gordon Coulton, St. Bernard, His Predecessors and Successors, 1000–1200 A.D. (Cambridge: The University Press, 1923) 62, vol. 1 of Five Centuries of Religion.

[2] Sir Arthur Bryant, The Age of Chivalry (Garden City: Doubleday and Co., Inc. 1963) 350.

[3] David Knowles, The Monastic Order in England (Cambridge: The University Press, 1940) 484–485.

[4] Knowles 482.

[5] J. Thomas Kelly, Thorns on the Tudor Rose: Monks, Vagabonds and Sturdy Beggars (Jackson: University Press of Mississippi, 1977) 28.

[6] Knowles 523.

[7] Knowles 525.

[8] Beverly Taylor, "Renaissance Music," The Winsor School, Boston, Fall 1978.

[9] Lowrie John Daily, Benedictine Monasticism: Its Formation and Development Through the Twelfth Century (New York: Sheed and Ward, 1965) 216.

[10] E. C. Butler, Benedictine Monachism: Studies in Benedictine Life and Rule (London: Longmans, Green and Co., 1919) 187.

[11] Daly 215.

[12] Knowles 405–406.

[13] Coulton 46.

[14] Bryant 349.

[15] Jocelin de Brakelond, The Chronicle of Jocelin de Brakelond, trans. Sir Ernest Clarke (London: Alexander Moring, The de le Mare Press, 1903) xxxviii.

[16] Bryant 350.

[17] Daly 224.

[18] de Brakelond xxxvii.

[19] de Brakelond 82.

[20] Butler 184.

[21] Benedict, The Rule of St. Benedict, trans. Cardinal Gasquet (London: Chatto & Windus, 1925) 10–11.

[22] Daly 231.

[23] de Brakelond 3–4.

[25] Butler 184.

[26] Benedict 119.

[27] George Gordon Coulton, The Friars and the Dead Weight of Tradition, 1200–1400 A.D., (Cambridge: The University Press, 1927) 13, vol. 2 of Five Centuries of Religion.

[28] Geoffrey Chaucer, The Canterbury Tales, trans. Nevill Coghill (Baltimore: Penguin Books, 1952) 29.

[29] Coulton, The Friars 12.

[30] Coulton, The Friars 13–14.

[31] George Gordon Coulton, The Medieval Scene: An Informal Introduction to the Middle Ages (Cambridge: The University Press, 1930) 75.

[32] Chaucer 29.

[33] Chaucer 30.

[34] Coulton, St. Bernard 394.

35 George Gordon Coulton, Getting and Spending (Cambridge: The University Press, 1936) 370, vol. 3 of Five Centuries of Religion.

36 de Brakelond 200.

37 Bryant 355.

38 Bryant 355.

39 Coulton, Getting and Spending 367.

40 Coulton, St. Bernard 392.

41 Daly 207.

42 Benedict 73.

43 Coulton, The Medieval Scene 19.

44 Benedict 73–74.

45 Bryant 351.

46 Coulton, St. Bernard 266.

47 Coulton, The Friars 95.

48 Friedrich Heer, The Medieval World: Europe 1100–1350 (Cleveland: The World Publishing Co., 1961) 41.

49 Daily 222.

50 Coulton, The Friars 175.

51 Benedict 85.

52 Heer 41.

53 Benedict 84.

54 Coulton, St. Bernard 266.

55 Coulton, St. Bernard 268.

56 Benedict 85.

57 Coulton, St. Bernard 524.

58 Kelly 8.

59 Coulton, St. Bernard 262.

60 Coulton, The Friars 95.

61 Giraldus Cambrensis, as quoted in Coulton, The Friars 96.

62 Coulton, The Medieval Scene 84.

63 Giraldus Cambrensis, as quoted in Will Durant, The Age of Faith (New York: Simon and Schuster, 1950) 786.

LIST OF ILLUSTRATIONS

(In the original paper the list of illustrations was placed after the contents. See Appendix B for the correct form for crediting illustrations.)

BIBLIOGRAPHY

Benedict. The Rule of St. Benedict. Trans. Cardinal Gasquet. London: Chatto & Windus, 1925.

Bryant, Sir Arthur. The Age of Chivalry. Garden City: Doubleday and Company Inc., 1963.

Butler, E. C. Benedictine Monachism: Studies in Benedictine Life and Rule. London: Longmans, Green and Co., 1919.

Chaucer, Geoffrey. The Canterbury Tales. Trans. Nevill Coghill. Baltimore: Penguin Books. 1952.

Coulton, George Gordon. The Friars and the Dead Weight of Tradition, 1200–1400 A.D. Cambridge: The University Press, 1927. Vol. 2 of Five Centuries of Religion.

———. Getting and Spending. Cambridge: The University Press, 1936. Vol 3 of Five Centuries of Religion.

———. The Medieval Scene: An Informal Introduction to the Middle Ages. Cambridge: The University Press, 1930.

———. St. Bernard, His Predecessors and Successors, 1000–1400 A.D. Cambridge: The University Press, 1927. Vol. 1 of Five Centuries of Religion.

Daly, Lowrie John. Benedictine Monasticism: Its Formation and Development Through the Twelfth Century. New York: Sheed and Ward, 1965.

de Brakelond, Jocelin. The Chronicle of Jocelin de Brakelond. Trans. Sir Ernest Clarke. London: Alexander Moring, The de la Mare Press, 1903.

Dickinson, John Compton. Monastic Life in Medieval England. New York: Barnes and Noble, 1961.

Durant, Will. The Age of Faith. New York: Simon and Schuster, 1950.

Heer, Friedrich. The Medieval World: Europe 1100–1350. Trans. Janet Sondheimer. Cleveland: The World Publishing Co., 1961.

Kelly, J. Thomas. Thorns on the Tudor Rose: Monks, Vagabonds and Sturdy Beggars. Jackson: University Press of Mississippi, 1977.

Knowles, David. The Monastic Order in England: A History of Its Development from the Times of St. Dunstan to the Fourth Lateran Council, 943–1216. Cambridge: The University Press, 1940.

———. Saints and Scholars: Twenty-Five Medieval Portraits. Cambridge: The University Press, 1963.

Taylor, Beverly. "Renaissance Music." A lecture given at the Winsor School, Boston. Fall, 1978.

Index